MYSTICS as a
FORCE for CHANGE

MYSTICS
as a
FORCE
for
CHANGE

SISIRKUMAR GHOSE

*This publication made possible with
the assistance of the Kern Foundation*

**The Theosophical Publishing House
Wheaton, Ill. U.S.A.
Madras, India/London, England**

2/12

Published by the Theosophical Publishing House, a
department of the Theosophical Society in America.

Library of Congress Cataloging in Publication Data

Ghose, Sisirkumar.
    The mystic as a force for change.

    Enlargement of: Mystics and society.
    "A Quest book."
    Includes bibliographical references and index.
    1. Mysticism—Addresses, essays, lectures.
I. Title.
BL625.G47   1981   149'.3   80-53954
ISBN 0-8356-0547-7   (pbk.)   AACR2

Printed in the United States of America

To
the memory of
Aldous Huxley

Acknowledgments

I owe a deep gratitude to Shri K. D. Sethna, editor, *Mother India*, for readily serializing these essays. Also to my friend, Shri Saumitrasankar Dasgupta, for his continued support, visible and invisible, while the work was in progress. Above all, to my mother who taught me the lore, the little that I have learnt.

Contents

Foreword

HOW should mystics be related to society? And what should society do about mystics?

The mystic-society problem is a limiting case of the more general problem of the individual and his culture. Like the pre-mystical modes of aesthetic and visionary consciousness, the mystical mode of consciousness is to some extent potentially in all of us. Normal waking consciousness is necessarily utilitarian, and its primary concern is survival and the avoidance of pain. But normal waking consciousness is not the only form of consciousness. There is also the aesthetic consciousness, for which the world is unimaginable beauty. There is also the visionary consciousness, for which the world is fathomlessly strange, enigmatic and unpredictable. And there is the mystical consciousness, for which the world is unity—the wisdom of the other shore whose other aspect is *mahākarunā*, the universal love. This 'other kind of seeing' is a faculty which, in Plotinus' words, 'all men have but few make use of'. In

what way does the culture, within which an individual has
been brought up, inhibit the actualization of his mystical and
pre-mystical potentialities? How and why does culture
prevent the great majority of individuals from making use
of those capacities for other kinds of seeing with which
they are endowed? These are the questions that confront
us.

Every culture is rooted in a language. No speech, no
culture. Without an instrument of symbolic expression
and communication, we should be Yahoos, lacking the
rudiments of civilization. It is because he starts by being
Homo loquax that man is capable of becoming *Homo
sapiens*. But this is a world in which everything has to be
paid for. Language makes it possible for us to be more
intelligent and better behaved than dumb brutes. But
whereas the dumb brutes are merely bestial, we loqua-
cious humans, who can talk ourselves into pure reason
and an almost angelic virtue, can also talk ourselves
down into being devils, imbeciles and lunatics. Our
destiny is ironically equivocal. Language and culture, the
sources of all civilization, the preconditions of law,
science, philosophy, poetry, religion, are also the preconditions of superstition, comic strips, magic and war, the
sources of all the collective and individual insanities that,
throughout recorded history, have been the contrapuntal
accompaniments of mankind's collective and individual
triumphs in the matter of intelligence and human-
heartedness. We are not only the beneficiaries of our
culture and of the language in which the culture is rooted;
we are also their somnambulistic or wildly intoxicated
victims.

Thanks to Dr. Ghose's wide reading and his gift of dis-
criminating selection, this book is, among other things, a
valuable anthology of texts, ancient and modern, Western and Eastern. All these texts, directly or indirectly,
refer to the mystic-society problem. One reads them with

respect and interest, sometimes with a grateful sense of having been vouchsafed a new insight. But gratitude, interest, and respect are mingled in all too many cases, with a certain impatience, a feeling of frustration. Why do terms employed have to be so vague? And why, if everyone is potentially capable of 'the other kind of seeing', is so little attention paid by the authors of the texts to the all-important problem of helping ordinary people in ordinary social situations to actualize their potentialities? Words like 'spirit', 'soul', and 'God' are too ill-defined to be helpful. Talk about the ineffability of mystical experience is perfectly correct, but requires to be related to a theory of language and a physio-psychology of the symbol-making, symbol-using mind-body. Retirement from the world and yogic practices within a group of like-minded individuals are certainly recommendable. But what about those for whom this sort of thing is not practicable? Ought not something to be done for *them*?

The philosophy of mysticism is a kind of transcendental operationalism. Perform certain operations, it teaches, and certain states of the mind-body may result. These states are experienced as being intrinsically valuable, and their fruits—improved character, increased sensitivity and insight—are often ethically desirable. These self-evidently valuable and socially useful states may be explained, on the symbolic level, in terms of some metaphysical or theistic hypothesis. But these hypotheses must never be taken too seriously. Nobody was ever saved or enlightened by assent to a proposition, only by an immediate experience on the non-verbal level. "What is called the teaching of the Buddha is not the teaching of the Buddha." "Why do you prate of God? Everything you say about Him is untrue." The teaching and the prating may encourage certain people to undertake certain operations which, in their turn, may result in the states of body-mind called 'mystical experience.' The value of the metaphysical or theistic words is merely instrumental; that of the experienced states is absolute, self-evident, and intrinsic.

The universe inhabited by acculturated human beings is largely home-made. It is a product of what Indian philosophy calls *Nama-Rupa* —'name and form'. Language is a device for de-naturing Nature and so making it comprehensible for human minds. The enormous mystery of existence, the primordial datum of an unbroken psychophysical continuity, is chopped up by the symbol-making mind into convenient fragments, to which verbal labels are attached. The labels and their logical (or illogical) patternings are projected into the outside world, which is then seen as a storehouse of separate, clearly defined and nicely catalogued things. Our names have created forms 'out there', each of which is an embodied illustration of some culture-hallowed abstraction. From the Christian 'prayer of simple regard' to the Zen Koan, from Wordsworth's 'wise-passiveness' to Krishnamurti's 'alert passivity' and 'awareness without judgment or comparison', all yogas have a single purpose—to help the individual to by-pass his conditioning as the heir to a culture and the speaker of a language. Mental silence blessedly uncreates the universe superimposed upon immediate experiences by our memories of words and traditional notions. Mystics are persons who have become acutely aware of the necessity for this kind of de-conditioning. Intuitively they know the essential ambivalence of language and culture, know that complete humanity and spiritual progress are possible only for those who have seen through their culture to be able to select from it those elements which make for charity and intelligence, and to reject all the rest.

Exceptionally gifted mystics in an exceptionally good environment will always find their way. What about ordinary people in ordinary social situations? How can these be helped to actualize their potentialities? We can begin by inculcating realistic notions about the nature of things in place of the inappropriate and outdated notions drummed into them by their cultural conditioning. Thus all young people can be taught something about the history of culture, something about the relationship between reality and symbol, something about the indispensable uses and fatal abuses of language. A person who knows that there have been hundreds of different cultures, and that each culture regards itself as the best, will not be inclined to take the boastings of his own culture too seriously. Similarly a person who has come to understand that labels are not identical with the things they are attached to, that words can be the most dangerous of narcotics and intoxicants will probably be cautious in speech and on his guard against the wiles of preachers, advertising men, and demagogues.

Such education on the verbal level requires, of course, to be supplemented by appropriate non-verbal training. Training in mental silence. Training in wise passiveness and choiceless attention. Training in sensitivity to other people's feelings and our own motives. Training in awareness of what, within ourselves and in the outside world, is actually happening, here and now, irrespective of what happened in the past and of the traditional notions connected with happenings of this particular kind. To work out a curriculum and a methodology for the non-verbal education of children and adults should not be too difficult. But whether the powers that be would ever permit such an education to be made gratuitous and universal is quite another question. The powers that be are at once the victims and the Machiavellian exploiters of all that is worst in their culture. They have a vested interest in the linguistic and cultural *status quo*—even in the *status* below *quo*. A population trained to make use of such 'other kinds of seeing' as the aesthetic, the visionary, and the mystical would be unmanageable by the traditional methods of narcotizing or inebriating propaganda. Mysticism *equals* misty schism *equals* subversion. In the eyes of the politicians and generals who control our destinies, it is most undesirable that the mass of humanity should be trained to see the world as beauty, as mysteriousness, as unity. It is in a culture-conditioned world of utilitarian values, dogmatic bumptiousness, and international dissensions that our rulers have come to the top; and that is the kind of world they would like their subjects to go on being conditioned to create for themselves. Meanwhile let us derive what comfort we may from the thought that other kinds of seeing are always there, parted from the normal waking consciousness (in William James's words) "by the filmiest of screens....Apply the necessary stimulus, and they are there in all their completeness.

Dr. Ghose's lucid and thought-provoking little book is a salutary reminder that, in spite of appearances to the contrary, all is never lost.

ALDOUS HUXLEY

Preface

THE series of seven, brief essays attempts little more than a restatement of a teasing theme: the relationship between the mystic and society. In some ways a privileged person, the mystic is also suspect. His very presence acts as a criticism and his absence is telling. We have not seen the last of him yet.

A complex of attitudes and experiences, mysticism is a way of life that has outlasted fashions in theory and revolutions in planning. If the mystical claim is at all right, the consequences of neglecting the intimations are fraught with danger. In a sense modern history, a long, almost deliberate deviation, proves the point. When all else has failed—or will fail—the mystics may be the only guides left to lead us out of the vicious circle of narrow, atavistic aims. They are with us even unto the consummation of the world. This poses a challenge for them no less. For the mystics too have now and then bogged; betrayed by alleys and byways, they have sometime mistaken a stage for a terminus. But always theirs is a way impossible to avoid, in the end perhaps the only way meant for the true becoming of man. As my American colleague, the poet, John Neihardt, had said to me the first time we met: Man without mysticism is a monster. A good summing up, I thought. The hand of Belial is everywhere.

Brief as it is, the book derives much of its material from several, secondary sources. This is not to suggest scholarship but that many voices, many cultures have taken part in the continuing dialogue, a dialogue pointing to a species of society higher than ours, a civilization of consciousness. Mysticism, less as a dogma and more as an enlargement of awareness, forces the honest thinker to re-think the human prospect in a world systematically threatened by the non-human and the anti-human. If these preliminary, exploratory essays, expressive of a point of view, can at all suggest the relevance of the mystical I shall feel rewarded. The limitations of the study are not unknown to me. Keeping out of the sieve of formulae I have not even properly defined mysticism. These essays must not be taken for an exposition of all the problems concerning mysticism, which will continue so long as man is man.

The book's main concern, perhaps to the point of an obsession, is to underline the social validity of mysticism. That is, the hypothesis that mystical psychology is a possible foundation for a viable society beyond anything known in the past, beyond religion and the monastery, if you like. Everything that rises must converge, Teilhard de Chardin used to insist. The task before us is to build the Earth, that too was one of his recommendations. The mystics may be the precursors of that emergent evolution. Talking of Mahayana, Evans-Wentz had played with the idea that one day the mystics might lead the rest towards a perfected social order. The how and why of this are worth exploring. In his *Commentary on the Proverbs* St.

Thomas Aquinas had pointed out the obvious: It is necessary for the perfection of human society that there should
be men who devote their lives to contemplation. The
words seem truer today than when they were written. To
domesticate the Manichean face of reality as of Two Cultures what other means do we have?

The main thesis or hypothesis may be stated briefly. In
terms of an ideal future, the true perfection, our present
achievements, spiritual and/or material, that appear to
us so real and impressive, turn out to be half-achieve-
ments, at best self-satisfied imperfections. There exists in
the various traditions, religious and otherwise, the hint of
another knowledge, another living. The double but related
crisis of civilization and evolution make its recovery both
likely and imperative. The impossible union of that knowledge and living—born and conditioned in another milieu—
with modern know-how becomes the aim and energy of
the future. Some of the developments of science seem to
point in this direction.

Without inwardness and criticism of outworn attitudes
the recovery is not going to happen. Whether this will
come through a slow or sudden change, through effort or
grace, the experience and experiment cannot obviously
depend on the outward means of the physical sciences
and a superficial psychology. A total perspective and
knowledge by identity—"self-awareness and all-aware-
ness by identity", vouched by the highest mystical knowledge—alone can dissolve the dualism which distorts our
perception and life-style and their overwhelming insignif-
icance. The evolution in ignorance calls for an evolution
in knowledge. Of this evolution the mystics are the first
mutants and martyrs. The change, or dying unto life, is at
once explosive and a fulfillment. As *Pratyabhijnyahri-
dayam* puts it, *balalabhe vishvamatmasatkaroti*, by acquiring the inherent power of awareness the aspirant
assimilates the universe within himself. And more: the

Gita speaks of the Self as the knower of the field in all the fields. Integrating the levels is a heroic task perhaps never before attempted or needed as much as today. Whether such integration can be generalized is the crux, the riddle before the collective yoga of mankind. Still this must be the higher dream, the ultimate issue.

In other words, and coming closer to our age, technology without transcendence will be a disaster. Its vice versa is no less true. Not, the, either/or but both/and is the way out, the verdict of the world court. Wisdom lies in balancing both demands, each with a justification of its own. Will the mystics and the scientists agree to build together? Or will their mutual allergy keep us perpetually maimed and self-divided? Whether many or few will respond to the challenge of the times as of an unfinished evolution, will decide our destiny, the secret purpose behind the workings of history.

The idea of the book originated, more than three decades back, in conversations with friends and students. It has been a slow growth but was completed, rather unexpectedly, during a teaching assignment in the States.

Aldous Huxley has done me a great kindness by readily writing a foreward. I deeply regret that it could not be published during his lifetime. The book is dedicated to him, for not only this but also other favors.

Sisir Kumar Ghose

Santiniketan (India)
August 15, 1980

I

What It Is

MYSTICISM has its own image of man and human destiny. Perhaps the best definition of man is that he is the possible. An exciting, inevitable awakening or self-discovery, mysticism, still in via, spells his second birth: the outer apparent man has to become the inner real man. To affirm himself is no doubt man's first business, but also to evolve and finally to exceed himself is part of the law of his being and becoming. This urge towards self-exceeding is not likely to die out of the race wholly or ever.

Instead of accusing the mystics of being dropouts and escapists, it might be fairer to say that in breaking the illusions of the cave dwellers they have been more responsible to the reality and the race. In the alchemy of awareness they have been the true scientists of catharsis and conversion, the piercing of the planes, which is another name for the ascent of man. The only radical thinkers, they alone go to the root of the matter, beyond the various shaky schemes of mundane perfection, swaying between the worship of the Fatted Calf and the horror of Organization Man. Of course in the evolution of consciousness, mysticism itself has to come of age and shed some of its individual and otherworldly emphasis.

A quest for a hidden truth in which all men can engage but few do, mysticism calls for an effort to understand, if not to co-operate. Union with the divine or the sacred for its goal, the mystical pointer to a non-physical element in man and the universe has the support of continuing experience or hypothesis. A breakthrough to the next higher development of man, the maturer forms of mysticism satisfy the claims of rationality, ecstasy, righteousness and a sense of the More. Without it a whole dimension of awareness would be missing and serious psychic disturbances predicted. Is not the malaise of the modern largely due to a neglect of transcendentals?

Not an elite mode of escape or religion without thought, mysticism is perhaps the only authentic life based on knowledge of the most adequate kind. Only it cannot be wholly expressed in words. At once praxis and gnosis, it reaches out to as it also recognizes the mystery and meaning of amphibian man. Described as personal religion raised to the highest power, the Establishment and mysticism do not get along too well. While for the most part validating religion, mysticism also transcends it; more free, it escapes the fetters of dogma, authority and organization.

Within man is the soul of the holy. And the sacred is really but a personified society. Rudolf Otto underlined the sense of the holy as a distinctive category of the religious or mystical apprehension. It is the 'otherness'—if not 'wholly other'—of the sacred that preserves the autonomy of the Absolute. Now and then the mystics have made claims of an unqualified union or communion with the deity or the Nothingness that is also the All; but generally a safe distance has been maintained between 'here' and 'yonder'. Else a hue and cry of heresy has been raised. Some religions, especially the Semitic, look upon pantheism with disfavor. But the Vedantic view, which insists upon the human-divine identity, is not exactly pantheism. All traditions have not been so liberal and some had to pay dearly for their truer conviction. To Calvin's ·double-edged query: "The Devil also must be God, substantially?" the unsuspecting Servetus had answered smilingly: "Do you doubt that?" The opinion cost him his life. The same fate was meted out to Mansur al-Hallaj for declaring what was not to be declared: *Anal Haqq* (I am the Truth). Whatever the theologians and the keepers of social morality might say, the experience of union, even unity, is undeniable. Mahmud Shabistari was not inventing when he said: "In God there is no duality. In that presence 'I' and 'we' and 'you' do not exist. 'I' and 'we' and 'you' and He become one. Since in the unity there is no distinction, the Quest and the Way and the Seeker become one."

The real presence of the sacred, *mysterium tremendum et fascinas*, mystery that repels and attracts, cannot be denied. By opting for the profane, the secular modern mind has unquestionably deprived itself, virtually created its own wastelands. Simply, the modern mind has exiled from its scheme two essential things: God or the Eternal and spirituality or the God-state. The mystic view, truer to heaven and home, is more sane and inclusive. As Plato held, the divine was the head and root of man. To which the Vedas might add that the root is within or above. Unlike the natural sciences which look only below and around, mysticism or spirituality dares to look above and within. Man has need of both: the knowledge of things as of self.

Mysticism shares common areas with magic, prayer, worship, science and metaphysics. It is based on the magical view of life; but though powers are known to exist, the true mystic has little interest in being a miracle man. Prayer and worship often form part—without being the essence—of the mystical complex. As for science, it is certainly verified knowledge. But since it is the science of the self that determines the aim as well as the method. Mysticism may take the help of metaphysics or theology but the help is not indispensable.

Mysticism has been variously defined. 'A consciousness of the beyond' should be generally acceptable, though this leaves out the nature of the beyond undefined. Man's denial of the Beyond is a denial of himself. Some have objected to the word 'mysticism' and would prefer 'enlightenment' or illumination. Others have pointed to similarities between prophetic religion, shamanism and mysticism. Similarities, not identities. Prophetic religions are generally action-oriented and have little or no inwardness. Shamanism, with its passion for the paranormal, communicates with worlds other than quotidian; but the content and practice of mysticism are different.

The higher forms of mysticism are distinguished by a loss of the separative consciousness: "Thou art That", "The knower and the known are one. God and I are one in knowledge." We may call it a third kind of knowledge, the two other being sense knowledge and knowledge by inference. This, by contrast, is knowledge by identity. But the abstract, intolerant intellect may miss the quality of love inherent in popular—but for that matter not lacking in profundity—or devotional forms of approach and experience, "a stretching out of the soul through an urge of love, an experimental knowledge of God through unifying love."

Obviously mystical experience has a wide spectrum. *Quot homines tot sententiae.* The Indian classification of knowledge [jnana], works [karma], and devotion [bhakti] is simple but basic. Each has its own field of operation and effectiveness; also each tends to be exclusive. At its highest, by suppressing the contents of the empirical consciousness, the way of knowledge moves towards an encounter with the naked All, the One without a second, the Fourth. As the *Mandukya Upanishad* puts it: "The Fourth, say the wise, is not knowledge of the senses, nor yet inferential knowledge. Beyond the senses, beyond all expressions is the Fourth. It is pure unitary consciousness wherein (all) awareness of the world and multiplicity is completely obliterated." By general consensus this is a borderland situation, the *ultima thule* of human consciousness.

This is when and how "the perishable puts on the imperishable." Here, perhaps, in the uncaused Cause, is the only guarantee of meaning, though not in an all-too-human sense. The feeling is not unknown to the scientists, for some of them have confessed to the peak experience. the biologist, Ludwig von Bertalanffy, finds no necessary opposition between the rational way of thinking and the intuitive experience. "In moments of scientific discovery I have an intuitive insight into a grand design." Without doing violence to reason, the dichotomy between science and mysticism may and ought to be healed.

Perhaps other dichotomies as well. For instance, the equation between mysticism and monasticism, the ascetic tendency to deny the world to find its reality, the open or implied denigration of life and matter. But if, as Sri Aurobindo holds, "All life is Yoga," the secret of the solution is yet to seek. The maturer forms of mysticism suggest not only an ascent but an integration.

The modern craze for instant vision through drugs is not likely to provide that. These pharmacological means for inducing visionary experiences are not new, except that they are now being manufactured by the irresponsible for the ignorant. Patanjali, an ancient Master of Yoga, mentions *ausadhi*, the Tantrics speak of wine, the Greek Mysteries used sedatives and stimulants for its initiates. As for the 'trips' that follow the use of mescalin, LSD, *cannabis indica*, hashish, etc., these are mainly extravertive, call for no discipline and do not achieve a permanent change in the personality. However intense and colorful, it is but a downward transcendence. Also the after effects can be risky. Such transcendence without tears, the parody may prove to be a costly way of getting something for nothing.

This cannot be the path to self-knowledge; indulgence is not the way to insight, to be "one'd with God", as *The Cloud of Unknowing* [1] put it. This identity is mysticism's final goal, a conscious return to the Root or Source. A sacral experience, it has its stages, what is called the Mystic Way. The journey, to which man is called, has been variously described: "Lead me from the unreal to the Real, from the darkness to the Light, from death to Immortality." The old prayer is for ever.

As this prayer will show, there are psychological and semantic hurdles in passage, from what is to what is not. if real, can be incalculable.
pierce the planes? The mystic world is riddled with paradoxes. The clash of categories can easily shatter logic; all the same it has the support of agelong experience. Though mysticism operates in a historical context, of here and now, it also readily reveals a timeless stance, beyond history. The Eternal Now releases us from the temporal tyranny, virtually from the limits of causation. The results of this release, if real, can be incalcuable.

As a cure for the provincialisms of the spirit, subtle and crude, there is nothing like mysticism. The true mystic, of whatever denomination, or no denomination, is a cosmopolitan. He was global before the phrase came into use. The teaching is universal whatever its origins. The essential unity of mystical experience does not mean a disappearance of diversities, or minute particulars, but that only the universal has a survival value.

The apotheosized field is the mystic's discovery and his real service to the life of the race. The wounds of separation will heal by no other means. As Thomas Merton saw it, the spiritual anguish of man has no cure but mysticism. Here is the only Reality-therapy that will endure, the truth that liberates.

Simply, the mystic is the sane or mature person. Though he will not allow anything, any inferior attachment, to come between him and the Real, he does not abjure all relations or responsibilities. Indeed, by his example he generates a set of altered relations and responsibilities which the enlightened reason cannot but endorse. The Way of the Cross and the Bodhisattva remain the highest achievements of a civilized consciousness. It will be suicidal to deny or ignore its value or reality. Mystical values may be difficult but not worthless. The highest of these is the birth of the psyche which, as Emerson pointed out, is the most important event in the life of Everyman. This altered state of awareness easily spreads out to include all things, bird and beast and man, all that exists, all that appears as the other. A solitary salvation satisfies neither the head nor the heart.

But the mystical is not all sweetness and light. Not always or altogether euphoric, the numinous has its dark side, the nether worlds not unknown to ancient explorers. Its a-moral undertone, beyond good and evil, has a touch of the absurd and the ominous. In that vast Ocean of Lila, as Sri Ramakrishna might say, our little doll of ego, logic and grammar can but melt and lose itself. Before such images as Kali and Rudra finitude collapses, the insulated universe is besieged by a ghostly frenzy which all may not be able to cope with, unaided. Reality is an ordeal and wisdom the pearl of great price. The blood-curdling Tibetan rituals and iconography can cause trauma in the unprepared soul. Such works of art as the Sphinx, Sung

7

paintings, Gothic cathedrals, Hindu temples, or *Missa Solemnis*, have been accredited conductors of the numinous. In fact, in the mystical universe nothing is trivial; everything can become a symbol pointing to the beyond; else there is a meeting of levels.

In that inner exploration or tense encounter there are moments when it becomes hard to distinguish being from its opposite. *Unio mystica* may seem to be but another name for *nirvana* or *fana*, both popularly equated with extinction. Assured of the deep secret of self-finding through self-loss, the mystics have heard the inner voice aright: "Annihilate yourself gloriously and joyously in Me, and in Me you shall find yourself; so long as you do not realize your nothingness, you will never reach the delights of immortality." From this arises the hope and justification of the alchemists: transmutation, a conversion or transformation of personality, in the image of God. Ideally, for the mystic, "the integrated quality of the cosmos itself is a hierophany." Deification, part of the dialectics of the sacred, is fundamental to orthodox Christendom as to Buddhism: Buddhas ye shall all become.

As we have seen before, mysticism is flanked by a semantic or communication hazard. The liberties and extravagances of the language of the mystics derive from the logical impossibility of having to describe the events or realities of one order in terms of another. Nicolas of Cusa, theorist of *coincidentia oppositorum*, union of opposites, firmly asserted that the walls of Paradise were built with paradoxes. God, held Heraclitus, was day and night, summer and winter, war and peace, hunger and satiety. Dionysius the Areopagite advised the seekers to "strip off all questions in order that we may attain a naked knowledge of that Unknowing and that we may begin to see the superessential Darkness which is hidden by the light that is in existent things." This is obviously not a common experience, ordinary knowledge or consciousness. How shall we know the *jimanmukta*, the free spirit? Again, how best may we render the Bodhisattva's Zenlike laughter that dissolves all logical distinctions as 'empty'? Yet whole cultures have been based on these insights or assumptions. True transcendence transfigures, a secret yet to learn. "God possesses all the attributes of the universe, being the universal Cause, yet in a stricter sense He does not possess them, since He transcends them all." How to regain the lost secret is a seminal, all-important question for the awakened soul, a question which contemporary culture has tried its best to avoid. The one-dimensional society is easily explained.

Luckily, there are teachers, prophets, incarnations to act as guides to the perplexed. The avatar's rationale is not hard to guess: God became man in order that man might become God. The God-man syndrome is the source of an abundant symbology. Since the soul is feminine, erotic or marriage symbolism should not surprise. The parallels between the Song of Solomon and the *lilas* of Radha-Krishna come to the mind. It is elementary knowledge that the 'Bridegroom-Word' is but the soul's return to the Lord of her seeking. The charge of obscenity has been loudest against the Tantras; for the pure in heart a different interpretation is, however, possible.

Another universal symbol has been that of the journey. The Mystic Way, *adhvara yajna*, the pilgrim sacrifice, to use the Vedic phrase, has been known as the Way of Return. According to Paracelsus, having lost the paradise of his soul man is a wanderer ever. In his *Conference of the Birds*,[2] Attar has described the seven valleys en route to the King's hidden palace: the valleys of quest, love, knowledge, detachment, unity, amazement and, finally, annihilation. As the Plenum-Void paradox will show, in the mystic dictionary annihilation equates amplitude or fulfillment. For *homo symbolicus* mysticism is an encyclopaedia of equations and correspondences, that partly reveal and partly conceal.

Mysticism's strength is clearly the strength of psychology in the original sense of the word. It is better to call it autology, the science of the self. The difference between the old and the new psychology has been well brought out by Ouspensky: "Never in history has psychology stood at so low a level, lost all touch with the origin and meaning, perhaps the oldest science and, unfortunately, in its most essential features, a forgotten science, the science of his possible evolution." Mysticism is the art and science of human becoming, his possible evolution.

It is only by its failure to distinguish between the abnormal and the supernormal that naturalistic science schools could dismiss mystical experiences *en tout cas*. For the positivist, secure in his self-assurance, mystical phenomenon is at best a religious sport. But as Rufus Jones had pointed out, as twentieth-century man knows it, psychology is empirical and possesses no ladder by which it can transcend the empirical order.

The mystics have, rather *are* the ladder, they have entire and varied disciplines for moving from one plane to the other. There is a science of the inner no less than a science of the outer. If man is a bridge the mystics are its engineers. Walter Hilton speaks of the Ladder of Perfection. The possibility of ranges of consciousness without thought is one of the basic premises of yoga and mysticism. It is an experiential refutation of the Cartesian dogma, *cogito, ergo sum*—I think, therefore I am. Being can exist without *cogito* or *ratio*. There can be a direct awareness of things where the self is its own evidence.

Outlasting fashions in thought, the evidence has by no means ceased. Admittedly difficult, raids on the inarticulate continue. Though expressions of the ineffable are bound to be conditioned and localized in terms of the

the milieu to which one belongs, there is a surprising consensus. These "people of the hidden" have a code of their own which sets them apart and makes for a kinship, a society within society. Here are creatures of circumstances who claim, from beyond history, a higher destiny. The mystic belongs to the Family of Man, and more than man, he has his comrades and is at home everywhere and nowhere. He alone has truly conquered alienation and looked into the heart of the human situation.

The present trends strongly suggest a dialogue between the men of the world, especially the scientists, and the men of spirit. The tendency of the times moves towards the ecumenism or ocean of tomorrow, towards a sane, pluralistic society. The convergence comes out strikingly in the works of Teilhard de Chardin and Sri Aurobindo, who have given a new turn to a great tradition. Both speak of an evolution of consciousness, do not consider organized religion as enough, are vitally concerned with collective salvation, a divine milieu. If the optimism is justified, they are indeed evangels of a new dispensation.

To modern mystics evolution is not ended. Pointing to a scale of senses, being and levels of the mind, some yet to be activized, mysticism provides a hope for man before which other forms of idealism, including short-term and pseudo-revolutions, are as nothing. With its abiding sense of the more and founded on psychological possibilities, mysticism may be the prelude to a sane society. It is a challenge rather than a comfort, an adventure than a hide-out.

The challenge is not for the well-adjusted and the other-oriented, the fixer and the climber, the dead souls for whom a life of sensations and conformity is enough. Some degree of maladjustment seems almost a prior condition. No wonder the mystics have been looked upon as great Outsiders, at best marginal men. That there should be a lunatic fringe among the brotherhood is not hard to understand. To opt for it one must have a call for holy living. He who seeks the Divine must consecrate himself to God and God alone.

For such people, in quest of self, God and meaning, the problem of communication is obvious. What shall they communicate and to whom? Speaking of that country, "the country of the soul," to those who live, contentedly, in this can never be easy. It is revealing that after he had been blessed with a spiritual experience St. Thomas Aquinas had said: "I have seen that which makes all that I have written and taught look small. My writing days are over." This from the author of *Summa Theologiae*[3] is not without its lesson. Even he would not or could not speak of "That".

Mystical revelation is no doubt solo, of a single or singular person. But could it not also be a redemption of both solitude and society? As Jacob Boehme said, in the mystic experience the world is not destroyed but re-made. Because of a persistent, exaggerated, otherworldly stress, the mystic has generally been treated, not unnaturally, as one who has undergone a deliberate civil death. But this is not and cannot be the whole truth. Action is not of one kind. The contemplative has a right to choose his own. "Sitting quietly, doing nothing," *wu-wei*, the contemplative does something that nobody else can. He keeps the channels open, actualizes possibilities of existence, represents attitudes and principles of charity, detachment and dedication which should govern inter-personal relations between men and nations. Only so can our "estranged faces" regain the serenity and at-homeness that should be the normal state of man. Not to learn from their life and example is to condemn ourselves as unteachable.

Mysticism is not an unexamined life and we should be able to see its relevance to the human situation, especially to the crisis today. Mysticism proves the individual's capacity to rise above the conditioning factors of nature, nurture and history, to achieve a third force which, if we only knew how, might change the basis and contour of our collective life. To say that it has not been a success so far is not enough. If the attempt has not succeeded, the incapacity or defection of the majority might be the main reason of the failure. Those who seem to be weak in history may finally shape it, because they are bound to the eternal order. "In Time they wait for the Eternal's hour."

Man's ultimate concern, mysticism proposes a revolution from above and by consciousness, *cetasa*. Without its aid futurology can only be a fantasy or an exercise in unqualified manipulation. To say "Technology is the grammar of the future" is dangerous nonsense. Technique and transcendence must learn to work together. That would be the beginning of the Total Man and Totality-thinking. And the individuals who will most help humanity in the hour of crisis are those who recognize a willed change from within as a step to a total change in our relationship with reality, the harmony of the whole. A Kingdom of Heaven within and a City of God without, the just society, remains one of mysticism's final gifts. Because he has acquired reason and still more because he has indulged his power of imagination and intuition, man is able to conceive of an existence higher than his own. It is to this dream and quest that he gives his final loyalty. His idea of God and Heaven is really a dream of his own perfection. An abiding and evolving truth, it is destined to fill a place in the future systems of thought, experience and aspiration. In darkness' core the mystics have dug wells of light; let us drink of it and be whole.

II

The Situation

Ping-ting comes for fire.
Suzuki, *Essays in Zen*

WAY back in 1920 Miss Underhill spoke of the strong need for re-statement with regard to institutional religions and mysticism. Today the need is even stronger and one is not surprised to find the redoubtable Toynbee, "reminded by the quickening touch of the Adversary," harking back to the same issue, the issue that is always the same. As part of the characteristic experience of the living generation in the Western world he had reached a point, he says, when "the question" 'What is your attitude towards religion?' was calling for an answer too insistently."[1] The question did not center round the destiny of a single individual or generation but that of an entire civilization on trial, to use another of his phrases. These are two evidences, out of many, and both point in the same direction — towards religion and mysticism, which is "personal religion raised to the highest power."

Nowadays one hears much about "return to religion" or even "return of religion." For a lucky few this has proved to be a lucrative proposition. But such a return to any credal conformity or hidebound institution will not solve our difficulties and is not the intended way out. It is more likely that mysticism is that way out, out of all compulsions and accidents of history into the freedom of the Spirit. As Marquette has pointed out, "In fact mysticism seems to be able to solve most of the dilemmas confronting our generation in nearly all the avenues of thought and activities. Hence the timely character of our attempt to study its modalities and to interpret whatever message it may have in store for puzzled modern man."[2] Or, in an earlier and somewhat different context, Meister Eckhart: "I am sure that if a soul knew the very least of all that Being means, it would never turn away from it." Whoever else has, the mystics have never turned away from it, "all that Being means." In fact, they have turned away from most other things that most men care for and turn to. That precisely is what has brought them in open conflict with all authoritarian systems. Between organized religion and mysticism the gap has been sometimes wide, even unbridgeable. Though a modern psychologist like Allport has told us that "the cultivation of mystical states . . . (is) a reasonable consequence of a thoroughly religious outlook," members of the church have been rarely so reasonable. An opposition, harsh or secret, at least minimal, has always been felt. Whether when mysticism throws off external authority altogether, it goes mad or not,[3] as a rule the two have not pulled on well. Leuba is perhaps a prejudiced observer where mysticism is concerned, but in this matter he seems to be right when he says: "In his search for God, the mystic goes his own way. If need be, he will brush aside formula, rites and even the priests who would serve him as a mediator. . . .Persons of this sort, harboring such convictions, may obviously be dangerous to the stability of any institution that has come

15

to regard its truths as the only truths, and its way of worship as the only way. And so it comes to pass that the more highly institutionalized are the . . . religions, the less tolerant they are to mystical piety when it rises beyond the ordinary." But such a permanent state of conflict can be hardly called ideal. Luckily, it has not always been so. Either institutions have been more tolerant, or the individuals less aggressive who, after a time, earned their role in the milieu.

In any case, it is too late in the day to force men to be free. (Pace dictatorships. Wahr matcht frei was the motto of the concentration camps, a very different type of concentration from what the mystics have known and recommended.) The growing impatience of progressive thinkers with sectarianism and form-bound religions suggests that a non-gregarious, non-contractual, non-compulsive association, with greater elbow room for the individual is the need of the hour. As Récéjac put it, "The Mystic City is without walls." No rigid or fixed formula, secular or monastic, can meet our complex needs. The Enclyclopaedia of Religion and Ethics says, a little gnomically, "Obedience and Rules cannot be imposed." That is, only a more plastic social and spiritual ordering than what politicians know, or can know, will meet that deep demand for an equation between the One and the Many—where all are different and all is one—which every society has attempted and none perhaps achieved.

However men may deny it or deny themselves, "Freedom is a capacity into which you are born, just as spacetime is a frame into which you are placed."[4] It is the inner dimension of our personality. The need for freedom—to grow, even to make mistakes—and the need for free variation, or "all roads", is too ingrained to be denied for long by any juggernaut of Establishment or Organization. Unfortunately, this is a sphere where "progress' is a demonstrable fact, where, thanks to organized lying, and heresy in high places, the scientific "nothing-but" explanations and the "historical necessities" of rapacious regimes, the last may well be the first. The tendency everywhere has been to force, to conform rather than to be free, with now all the additional help received from applied science. And this often in the name of freedom itself. But, as the wise have always known, "The heart of so great a mystery cannot be reached by one road only," certainly not by the narrow lane of doctrines and rigid religious groups. When the Devil wants to spread confusion, it has been said, he starts an institution. It will be foolish to deny the need and usefulness of religion, but it is a means and not an end. As Vivekananda once said, it is good to be born into a religion, it is bad to die in it. Whatever else religion has done, it has not changed human life and society, at least not brought about that complete change which is the heart of the mystic promise and effort down the ages. Defending the churches Underhill said, "Man needs a convention, tradition, a limitation if he is not to waste his creative powers; and this convention the mystics find best and most easily in the forms of the church to which they belong." One can only ask: Do they really? In any case, after a time men have also felt the need to break conventions and open new ways of the Spirit, lest one good custom corrupt the world. The great religions themselves would have been impossible without this mystic core, inevitable but unpredictable, for who shall set a limit for the workings of the Spirit? It bloweth where it listeth.

It is also a fact that in trying to rule rather than bind society, most religions have more or less compromised with questionable, recalcitrant, even unspiritual elements. They could not always insist, except in a manner of speaking which no one need take seriously, on that inner change of the whole being which is the essence of religious living; they had to be content with credal adherence, a formal acceptance of ethical standards and conformity to institution, ceremony and ritual. But this, by itself, cannot transform the race, it has not; it cannot create a new principle of human existence, such as the poets and prophets have dreamt of and which is perhaps the secret purpose presiding over our evolution. A total spiritual direction given to the whole of life and the whole of nature alone can lift humanity beyond itself. Only a few mystics have known and tried that. Will or can the rest follow?

At first sight this insistence on a radical change might seem to put off all hope to a distant future. Even if that were so, it would still remain the sole possibility. For, as Sri Aurobindo says truly, "To hope for a change of human life without a change of human nature is an irrational and unspiritual proposition. What is necessary is that there should be a turn in humanity felt by some or many towards the vision of this change, a feeling of its imperative need, the sense of its possibility, the will to make it possible in themselves and to find the way. That trend is not absent and it must increase with the tension of the crisis in human world-destiny; the need of an escape or solution, the feeling that there is no other solution than the spiritual solution cannot but grow and become more imperative under the urgency of critical circumstance. To that call in the being there must always be some answer in the Divine Reality and Nature."[5] There, in brief, is the hope and the faith, to which some have always responded or something in man has always responded. As even modern physics now tells us, bigness is no index of psychological force. The few will "save the city."

However few, the mystics lift human history into a new dimension and provide it with this adventure of ideas and more than ideas. Mysticism, the art of union with Reality, is not played out. Even to C. S. Broad, usually a cautious thinker, it seemed "more likely than not that in mystical experience men come into contact with some Reality or some aspect of Reality which they do not come into contact with in any other way."[6] The game has but begun, with new rules and dénouement.

Throughout history, the free have spoken with one voice. The verdict has not only been unanimous but complementary and self-correcting. That it has a bearing on our time of troubles only the pervert and the deliberately blind will deny. The present work was undertaken in the belief that a re-statement, however brief and fragmentary, of mystical theory and practice, might bring home to us some principles or conclusions that have weathered the storm of centuries and still stand, as pointers, to tease us out of thought as doth Eternity. They can still help us to build on surer foundations. Of what we have instead, the Persian proverb has the last word, "If the first building-stone is askew, the structure may reach to the heavens, and all of it be crooked." Whether it reaches the heavens or the moon it can but be the same, an extension of fearful folly. Who among us has not felt an occasional misgiving about the direction of modern history, of these our "warfare states", the possibility, the eagerness, and now the proven ability to wipe out large masses of men and land areas at a stroke or in a second? Genocide is now taken for granted, almost as casually as one takes a tablet of aspirin to cure a common headache. Most of our thinkers, artists and "disinherited minds" have felt the shadow of racial suicide descend on the human stage. As Dean Inge had noted long back: "There has never perhaps been a time when the sense of doom has been so widespread."[7] Yes, and with such good reason! The agony of extremity as well as the failure of popular panaceas have forced men to look for help everywhere, in unlikely places. But there is little hope anywhere, at best false hope,—except among the mystics. They alone have fought the inner battle and won. How can we socialize that victory.?

Some at least have felt that the mystics, a neglected and misunderstood minority, may have a knowledge and technique that could save us from impending disaster. This will be a test for both mysticism and the modern age. Obviously it will not be a magical remedy, something to be applied from the outside, nor will it run according to any formula. As Alexis Carrel put it with some force: "We will not establish any program. For a program would stifle living reality in a rigid armor. It would prevent the bursting forth of the unpredictable, and imprison the future within the limits of our mind."[8] There is also no guarantee that it will succeed. Who knows, the mystic might succeed by using the piercing paradox of apparent failure, the "divine technique" of affliction, as Simone Weil once said? The mystic is not unfamiliar with nor adverse to the call of supreme sacrifice. As Karl Jaspers has recently insisted, "Sacrifice remains the foundation of true humanity. If its soldierly form disappears, it will assume others. . . .The great renunciations are not only necessary to save a free world but also to bring men back from a life lost in an empty consumer's existence after a few hours of unrelished work. Sacrifice would not only make peace possible; it would fulfil it."[9] In the words of Lecomte du Noüy: "The martyrs represent one of the most powerful levers of humanity. . . .That is why governments are usually careful not to 'make martyrs'. . . .Who knows if Christianity would have developed had Jesus not been crucified?" Again, "The human flock obeys an obscure order: it must rise, it cannot do without a leader. Thank God, if there have been evil influences, they have been counteracted, on an average, by that of certain rare, privileged men, comparable to the transitional animals who were in advance of their time. These men attained a higher stage of evolution. . . .Strange to say, in spite of their handicaps, of the fact that the doctrine they taught was less pleasant and demanded sacrifice it is they who gained the higher prestige in history, and their teachings outlasted and out-shone all the others."[10] Mysticism is stern stuff and it can do without propaganda. The case for mystics can stand by itself, on surer grounds of the Being, if only one has the courage and the capacity to verify what they have to say and what their presence implies. This calls for a revision of modern errors and heresies, a revolution in thought. If, as the Buddhists hold, we are the result of all that we have thought, it is time to change our thought. If our times are out of joint, a psychologist has told us, it is because they are *philosophically* out of joint. If we are to set them right, we shall have to set them *philosophically* right.[11] The mystics invite us to that mental spring cleaning.

The metaphysical barbarities of a few centuries are perhaps endurable agony, the inevitable price to be paid for the hindsight that is another name for wisdom, wise after the event. But to admit mysticism, it is not necessary to give up our gains from science. That is a popular mistake. In 1950 Einstein had spoken of "a new way of thinking if mankind is to survive." This "inner road to salvation" was more explicitly stated by another thinker speaking of "The idea of the goal of a conquest of con-tradictions, which involves a synthesis encompassing both rational understanding and the mystical experience of unity, as the explicit or implicit mythos of our own present time." There need be no quarrel between science and spirituality. Mysticism itself is as much a knowledge as feeling, there is more of knowledge in it than many suspect. It is a *vidyā*, or science; it is *ekavidyā*, the knowledge of the One or the knowledge that unites or reconciles the different sides of existence; above all, it is *Brahmavidyā*, the knowledge of the One Self, one in all, In the House of Self there are many mansions and in the Garden of God many games to play other than Darwin, Marx or Freud knew of. For this all that we have to do is to admit degrees of knowledge and levels of understanding. The laws of one plane do not hold good on another—how much correction in that simple truth!

The hard shell of materialism is cracking, both from within and without, with the crack of doom. When scientific atomization and manslaughter reach satanic proportions it is perhaps time to cry halt—and point out, plainly, the diabolic potentialities of our own Mechanomorphism. In exorcizing the devils of industrialism and the insane ideological conflicts that tear the world's heart apart, we may have to return, humbly, to the age-old insights of the mystics. This book could not have been written without that hope and faith, a certain belief in mysticism and its possible application to the problems of our day. "The enclosed life is the ancient form of religious life . . . and will always be the most modern,"[12] says one who has embraced it willingly with open eyes. The enclosed life, of an apparently separate community is always a strategic necessity, the necessity to concentrate. It is not an exclusive club. As we shall see, the Order of Mystics is not an ancient luxury or refuge for a maladjusted elite, "outworn ideas of a bygone age, or at best religious poetry"; it is a way of life, everlasting life, always extending in new directions, always capable of fresh formulations. The Infinite is not exhausted, it is eminently adjustable to our overdramatized *Angst* and the *avant-garde* theater of the Absurd, perched above the Abyss.

The mystics have a right to be heard, though they themselves might not claim it, because both their insight and their criticism are part of First Principles, modern man's major omission. Also because they have lived out what they talk about. Those who fail to practice, said Wang-Yang Ming, also fail to understand. The mystics practice what they preach. If they speak with authority it is because they know what they are talking about and they don't double-talk. Through their images and parables, their doctrine, above all through their examples shines

the clear imprint of experience and an appeal that
neither custom nor age has been able to stale. Whether it
is Lao-Tse returning upon the Black Ox or Thomas Merton
telling us of "the silence of the far mountains on which the
armies of God and the enemy confront one another in a
mysterious battle, of which the battle in the world is only
a pale reflection" or Sri Aurobindo speaking of a spiritual
evolution,[13] it is the same voice. For the sake of safety and
sanity, if not salvation, why not listen?

> We know the truth has been
> Told over to the world a thousand times;
> But we have had no ears to listen yet
> For more than fragments of it; we have heard
> A murmur now and then, an echo here
> And there.

III

An Approach

*Who are these men and what are
these words they speak?*

"ATTEMPTS are sometimes made to have done finally with questionings which have so often been declared insoluble by logical thought[1] and to persuade men to limit their mental activities to the practical and immediate problems of their material existence in the universe; but such evasions are never permanent in their effect. Mankind returns from them with a more vehement impluse inquiry or a more violent hunger for immediate solution. By that hunger mysticism[2] profits and new religions arise to replace the old that have been destroyed or stripped of significance by a scepticism which could not satisfy because although its business was inquiry it was unwilling sufficiently to inquire."[3] Thus spake Sri Aurobindo.

In other words, mysticism can change, it cannot die. When everything else fails, or will ultimately .fail, it stands its ground. Our extremity is God's opportunity. Amid the disasters of our own time, more eyes are turning towards it as the only way out. Modern man, as Jung put it, is in search of his soul. Of that search mysticism is both cause and goal, of this deeper finding and possibility the mystics have been pioneers ever. But what, precisely, is the possibility and whom does the mystic seek? Briefly, and paradoxically, the mystic seeks himself, to know himself. Our search for the Self is moved by the Self. "Yes, 'Know Thyself' is still the key to wisdom ... and this self-knowledge as developed in Hindu psychology," says an exponent of one school of mysticism, "is the way to freedom, truth and harmonious living."[4] The injunction: "Know Thyself" carries with it the suggestion that we probably do not know ourselves, or not sufficiently. A working knowledge we all have, often that is all we have, but rarely the much more that we need to know and become. To become what we are, that is what the rare man, the mystic, seeks. "No one can teach another how to acquire it."[5] But, as Evelyn Underhill tells us, this is "an innate tendency of the human spirit towards complete harmony with the transcendental order. . . . I believe this movement to represent the true line of development of the highest form of human consciousness."[6] How to acquire this? Luckily, the intelligent being, if he so likes, carries within him the wherewithal to surpass himself.[7]

But, as we have just now said, the knowledge or experience is essentially solo. No one gives it to another.

"I am told that you possess the pearl of divine knowledge; either give it to me or sell it to me."

"I cannot sell it for you have not the price thereof, and if I give it to you, you will have gained it too cheaply. You do not know its value. Cast yourself headlong, like me, into this ocean in order that you yourself may find the pearl."[8]

The history of this human seeking or becoming is man's true history as it is also the secret burden of his existence.

The saints and seers, of all ages and countries, known and unknown, bear testimony to this endless adventure of man. This is the journey of journeys, of man and Magi. So far such men, the yogis and mystics, have been a rarity, stars that mostly dwelt apart, but they need not be so aloof and such oddities for all times. As even a critical observer could not help saying: "Alas! quixotic enough sometimes" mysticism is "one of the most significant chapters of the history of humanity.[9] In a sense of course "All life is yoga" and it is not impossible to imagine a community where the mystic impulse and effort are not only better understood but form a normal part of the social setting. If this ever happens, the treasures of the spirit, or what we have called mysticism, might prove to be of greater worth than what most of us have allowed ourselves to imagine. Mysticism which has been usually treated as an egocentric, abnormal, escapist[10] activity, is in fact an escape from the ego and an encounter with the totality of experience, or Reality. As its concern is with the Real, and the "need to be real," it must be held to be a realizable ideal in both our individual and collective life, provided that we are prepared to pay the price, that is, fulfill the conditions. The Buddha has described the nature and result of acquiring such a new center of personality, *Brahmavihārā*, thus:

"Do not deceive each other, do not despise anybody anywhere, never in anger wish anyone to suffer through thy body, words or thoughts. Like a mother nourishing her only child with her own life, keep thy immeasurable loving thought for all creatures.

"Above thee, below thee, on all sides of thee, keep on all the world thy sympathy and immeasurable loving thought, which is without obstruction, without any wish to injure, without enmity.

"To be dwelling in such contemplation while standing, walking, lying down, until sleep overcomes thee, is called living in Brahman."

Who will say that the ideal is not real or that it is not needed today? Perhaps today more than ever before. But today is everyday. That also is part of the wisdom. What will be the nature of such a life, today, we cannot foresee, much less demand. Obviously much that is normal to our present ways of seeing and living will no longer be so. One is however permitted to think that the difficulties of a slow and painful evolution in the midst of which we find ourselves will turn out to be a test and an opportunity and find their justification. And though it may be the hard way, in the end there will be no other. But when one thinks of the complexities of our present social and intellectual Organization Man the yoke of the mystics is light indeed.

Mysticism, which is the heart of religion, is always attempting an answer to the old, agonizing question: What is Man? As one looks around, above, below and within, one sees life as the first mystery of our existence, life occult and vibrant in an otherwise dead and inert universe. But it is not till mind appears on the scene that the mystery becomes a problem. The thinking reed is miserable because it thinks. Till the time he can open or overpass himself in a consciousness more than the mental, the son of man has no rest in his wanderings in the Valley of False Glimmer, the labyrinths of illusion, unreality and appearance. In a sense all problems begin and end with the mind, which has sometimes been called a reality-killer.

Leaving such metaphysical ideas aside, the problem that weighs most with modern humanity is the just accommodation of its scientific technique with a rational organization that will make life worth living for the vast majority, which at present it clearly is not. There ·is nothing unusual or unnatural about the attempt, except perhaps the manner of it, which is the reason why it has failed. The issue is plain: What is the truth or nature of things and how are we to embody it in our social living?

This has been a human concern throughout all history and in the attempts at solution men have experimented with every form of social reasoning and social organization. Yet the amount of human misery remains much the same and human nature perhaps as unregenerate as ever. Is history, then, a vicious circle? Endgame?

In a mood of enforced sobriety we begin to wonder if there has not been some gap or lacuna, some miscalculation somewhere, a fatal weakness in our equipment or Achilles' heel. Maybe we have not been so much sinful as ignorant. But, of course, the sin of pride has been there always. Since the days of the Renaissance there has indeed been a boom in the pride industry.

> But man, proud man,
> Dressed in a little brief authority,
> Most ignorant of what he's most assured,
> His glassy essence, like an angry ape,
> Plays such fantastic tricks before high heaven
> As make the angels weep.

But most ignorance is vincible and the ape may be teachable, at least some have been. Amid the clash of slogans and competing panaceas, all in full panoply, the voice of conscience or the time-spirit seems to point to ends and means which we have neglected and left aside as unimportant and inessential. The stone which the builders rejected is now become the cornerstone. Mysticism, often "shy to illumine", may yet be the light we need, the light we lost. For we are no longer fooled or hypnotized by the limited and ignoble ideals of the economic or the psychotic man, by unethical technological progress, by the regimented State or the "Big Brother", with his big stick of lying propaganda, war and revolution, and total destruction. To accept or acquiesce in these pernicious versions of necessity and progress—and the low idea of human nature on which these seem to be based—is to accept the part for the whole, the end of man. It can lead us only into deeper difficulties. To the prophets of such violent and collective cure one can only say: You are not the doctor but the disease.

It is exactly here that mysticism, almost never tried as a social experiment, except in closed and curious communities, opens up a new prospect. It is the utility of yoga, Sri Aurobindo has said, that it opens to us a gate of escape out of the vicious circle of our ordinary human existence, brings a ray of hope into the darkness of our fallen existence.[11] Sheer force of circumstances compel us to face and look for help to the community of saints and seers, yogis and mystics whom we had so long cheerfully, even enthusiastically, given short shrift, neglected during the Age of Reason, which has so readily now turned into an Age of Anxiety. History which has been largely played around the Odd Man Out theme may yet find its savior. Today there is no justification to continue the old blissful ignorance about mystics and mysticism. We have, in self-defense if for no other reason, to take note of their experience, doctrine, or metaphysics, their psychology and, if one may say so, their sociology. Or perish. To refuse to listen to them is not advisable. That many of our thinkers—Gerald Heard, Aldous Huxley, and Pitirim Sorokin, among others—should seem to echo or speak in terms of mystical insight, analysis and approach is not surprising. Perhaps there never was an age more open to these ideas. We are probably moving towards a Yogi Age.

Among recent works which focussed attention on the subject—mainly perhaps because of a catchy title—is *The Yogi and the Commissar* by Arthur Koestler. According to him, the issues of modern life depend upon two types of people or attitude, between what he calls Change from Within and Change from Without.[12] Both have their dilemmas. At the end of his book Koestler confesses,

"Neither the saint nor the revolutionary can save us; only the synthesis of the two. Whether we are capable of achieving it, I do not know." Naturally, he does not, being neither. (His later researches show him to be completely unfit for the undertaking.) On the nature of the synthesis he has little to say except to use the word. The need for it, however, is more crucial than an intellectual flirting with ideas could ever indicate. Unless, therefore, the human race is to fall by the wayside, it must seek the synthesis. Of course one is not to expect a fiat, an easy, magical victory. There may be more hardships, of readjustment, than we can imagine. After all, the way of the mystics is largely one of self-mortification and crises of decision, it involves an ardor and austerity of the spirit which it would be foolish to minimize. The ancient seers did not exaggerate when they spoke of the Way as sharp as the razor's edge, difficult of going, hard to traverse, *Ksurasya dhārā niśhitā duratyayā*. It is also possible that mysticism, as we have known it in the past, might change its forms, or some of its forms, beyond recognition. But, always, it will be a variation on the same theme, of man at his highest.

To the question: "How can the mystics help and what have we to learn from them?" it can be safely pointed out that what the mystics have to give us is a profounder self-knowledge and world-knowledge, an integral view of existence most likely to preserve us from our present pitfalls. The mystics see clearly, correctly and comprehensively. As *Theologica Germanica* points out, "Now the created soul of man has also two eyes. The one is the power of seeing into eternity, the other of seeing into time and the creatures." The mystic uses both eyes, if not all mystics, at least the greater ones who have seen the deepest into the life of things and the mysteries of integration. Nor is their insight a product of their social ineptitude and unawareness. On the contrary, as Simone Weil has shown, to contemplate the social scene is as effective a purification as to withdraw from the world. It is only the terms of reference that are different. The mystic is as much interested in man as anybody. In fact, he has more to offer. So, we can add, the art and science of contemplation, as mysticism is usually referred to in the West, will show, among other things, the interrelation of God, Nature and Man.

Briefly, the mystics, or contemplatives, will help us in at least four related and useful ways: they will correct our inadequate world-view; they will point out the right methods for making this world-view effective in our lives; this they will do, not by any "escape" (one word too often profaned) from life but by adding to it; finally, they will do this not in the life of the individual alone but also in the life of the group or society as a whole. Incidentally, they will correct the fallacies and limitations of the technique of violent revolutions, and our obsession with matter and physical force as the only weapon or "midwife" of social change. A survey of mysticism, honestly carried out, is likely to provide us with hope and understanding, and a course of action that alone makes sense and has a right to succeed, however long the labor.

Some of the functions of the mystical attitude and experiment cannot help being negative or purgative. But on the whole its direction and result will be positive. Mild-eyed but vigilant (while others slept), the "sleepless ones" help to keep the world "disinfected," as Aldous Huxley once put it, with the help of a detergent formula. "The mystics," he said, "are a channel through which a little knowledge of reality filters down to our human universe of ignorance and illusion. A totally unmystical world would be a world totally blind and insane." The mystic, truly understood, puts back more into society, than any other individual or group. As Bennett has suggested, mysticism represents "a type of mind . . . which the institution does not and cannot produce . . . Yet while it cannot produce, it can and must make use of the radical. Its very life depends on so doing. The institution which affects to see in him an enemy is excommunicating one who is fitted to keep in touch with the renewing sources of its own life."

These are, it will be seen, large claims which this essay cannot hope to "prove" or substantiate. The truths we are dealing with are largely self-evident or nothing. But men have been blessed with the right to refuse, to say "No" to a Christ or a Buddha. The freedom is still freely used. We shall be content if we can provide a possibility, presumption or hypothesis, if we can raise the old questions, questions which we ignore at our peril. For our part we admit the actuality of a unitive truth, of a Knowledge, more self-fulfilled, or revealed, as some would say, than this our all-too-human knowledge, "this limited consciousness in whose narrow borders we grope and struggle." Further, we take our stand that spiritual evolution is a fact, perhaps the most important fact about us. From this it follows that a community of saints or gnostic beings, sādhúnām rājyam, or a Kingdom of Heaven upon Earth, is a realizable ideal and must one day be realized. The future belongs to the mystics, not as a sect but as an image of man to be. Microcosm of the macrocosm, man starts from animal vitality and its activities but a self-fulfilled divine life is what he is secretly after, his true objective. The mystics have been usually credited with the technique of deliverance or escape from the wheels of becoming, saṁsāra, into some ineffable Nirvana or the heavens beyond. They may yet prove to be the architects of the "rainbow bridge marrying the soil to the sky," amṛtasya setuh. Craftsmen of the divine plan, they carry with them the nisus of the deity within and the tools of the transition, in theory as in practice. Yoga is praxis, nothing if not skill in works, as Krishna says. The mystics always emphasize the need for seeing clearly and for self-exceeding instead of muddling through or whirling about the mud and filth of assertive egos, dictatorships, plutocratic or proletarian, or the tepid democracies of shopkeepers with nothing high or ideal to sustain them for long except as an endless game for politicians and the worldly-minded to play, since they know no other. Yoga or mysticism is a know-how like any other to deliver us from the damnation of our unprincipled ways. We have not seen the last of it yet.

The need for such an ideal as the mystic's, of self-finding through self-exceeding, is likely to be questioned by the modern mind. There is virtue in honest doubt. The doubt or question touches upon such ideas as those of evolution, civilization, science, and the techniques for heightening individual and social behavior. Let us take each of these briefly, and see what mysticism has to offer.

First, the mystics break through the *cordon sanitaire* of biology. While poets, like Whitman, talk of a "mystical evolution" the mystics know. To them Spirit and Matter appear as poles of the same Existence. The theory is simple, not so the living out of it. As one of them puts it: "We speak of the evolution of Life in Matter, the evolution of Mind in Matter, but evolution is a word which merely states the phenomenon without explaining it. For there seems to be no reason why Life should evolve out of material elements or mind out of living forms, unless we accept the Vedantic solution that Life is already involved in Matter and Mind in Life, because in essence Matter is a form of veiled Life and Life a form of veiled Mind Consciousness. And then there seems to be little objection to a farther step in the series and the admission that mental consciousness may itself be a form and a veil of higher states which are beyond the Mind."[13] This, briefly, is the mystical view, intellectually stated, that "along with the mental evolution of man there has been going forward the early process of another evolution", of the soul and the spirit in him. As Lecomte du Noüy has tried to show, "Evolution is not ended." The mystics are the "transitional forms", and "Man must fight to prepare the advent of the spiritual being he is destined to become." This is a "test on the psychological plane." Earlier, as a result of evidence collected from far and wide and experiments carried out, F. W. H. Myers was led to the conclusion that "Man is in course of evolution; and the most pregnant hint which these nascent experiments have yet given him is that it may be in his power to hasten his own evolution in ways previously unknown."[14] But, it must be said, the mystic does not merely state, he does not speculate, he experiences. He has first verified, in personal experience, what he is saying, "reading the text of without from within." He is specially equipped for the task, and it is in terms of his inner vision and a cosmic background that we must look upon human evolution, its past, present and future, upon history and civilization, and every attempt at organized life. All our values are values of civilization, they emerge from and replenish the common stock. What is the share or contribution of the mystics to the common stock? Or are they, as has sometimes been heard, merely enjoying privileges, which they have done little to earn or to produce? Are they parasites? And do they not, the objection goes on, with their uncertain and unverifiable lights, disturb the common man and his *dharma*, the *dharma* of his civilization? Some of the "characteristic objections" against mysticism have been: That it is not real knowledge; that it has no social usefulness; and that such knowledge does not exist anywhere. But the objections lose their edge from the fact that those who make them are not and have never been mystics themselves. As regards the mystic claim, of leading the community along the path of Light, did they not have, the critics add, a long time to deliver the goods? Are not spirituality and social progress mutually exclusive: Either/or?

But the pragmatic test, so crudely put, is not a valid test for either the mystic experiment or evolution. To quote Eckhart: "Some people want to see God with their eyes as they see their cow, and to love Him as they love their cow—for the milk and cheese it brings them. This is how it is with people who love God for the sake of outward wealth or inward comfort. They do not love God who love him for their own advantage." Or, as Brother Lawrence has it: "Let us not amuse ourselves to seek or to love God for any sensible favors (how elevated soever) which He has done or may do us. Such favors, though never so great, cannot bring us near to God." That also is a lesson our age might learn, an age that has begged the God of Machine for favors, fair and foul. And got what it wanted.

The mystic's real task or service to the race is not so much to help men solve problems in their all-too-human ways as to transcend secular and humanistic values, to transfigure them in the light of the spiritual ideal or the will of God. The mystic brings not peace but the sword—of discrimination—and a sense of the holy, the sacramental attitude in all the ways of one's being. Very few civilizations approximate to that ideal. Are mysticism and civilization working at cross purposes, then? No, not necessarily. The mystics have played an important, an enormous part in the making of man and civilization. Most early civilizations owe a good deal to this creative minority. In the absence of a sharp division of labor, such as has marked the later periods of our history, the early mystics would also be among the priests and medicine-men of the tribe. (The role is neither extinct nor anachronistic. Incarnations of the devil are equally available; in fact, more.) Also, beneath the careful and elaborate disguise of initiation rites, of symbols and mythologies, there was not only a belief but a knowledge, pre-logical or not. This idea of an age of mystical intuition or knowledge, at least in a few, before the full growth of reason or intellect the modern mind finds hard to accept. But the evidence of facts points otherwise. In *Primitive Man As Philosopher* Dr. Radin has pointed out, "Orthodox ethnology has been nothing but an enthusiastic and quite uncritical attempt to apply the Darwinian theory of evolution to the facts of social experience." The result of such an uncritical activity, he has suggested, is that no progress in understanding will be achieved unless scholars rid themselves of the curious notion that everything possesses a history à la Darwin.

If the mystics enjoyed an importance and were regarded as respected members of the community it was because they spoke with authority. That this authority was now and then abused or mixed up with local and infra-spiritual values, need not surprise any one. It only shows that the mystic is not, *ipso facto,* a transformed being in every way, also that it is never easy to mass-produce spiritual values. (In his "catalogue of faults" Cassian had noted: gluttony, fornication, vainglory and pride, anger and accidie. Marxists and Freudians could no doubt add a few more.)

Gradually, perhaps because society proved to be delinquent or unwilling or unable to cooperate, the men of God broke away from the men of the world, and a kind of dichotomy has prevailed since then. Hocking has called this "world flight". So began the withdrawal of the wise and the ascetic to the margins of society. From the center they moved on to the periphery and there, for the most part, they have dug themselves in. For instance, it was not St. Anthony's aim, we are told, to reconcile Christianity with culture but to "keep them apart." Eastern parallels to this holy *apartheid* are easily suggested. It is clear that the mood of asceticism and other-worldliness had a large share in this movement towards isolation. There might also have been the expediency of a separate community given entirely to religious and spiritual seeking or experiment. Instead of unduly interfering with or being interfered with by the less evolved life around them, the mystics preferred to cultivate their own garden. This they did as trustees, so to speak, and as a rule they have been willing to impart their knowledge and way of life to all those whom they considered fit for such instruction. They were perhaps not exactly democrats, in the sense that they did not accept the idea that anyone who chose to think himself fit became fit by that act of faith or presumption. The salvation of every one is assured, that is the larger hope. But there is the time factor too, and the fitness of the candidate depends, as the Indians might say, on his past *karma* and *saṁskāra*, the stream of his action and tendencies, his temperament. It is an open question whether the mystics were not justified in so confining and concentrating their activities within small communities or whether our political bosses of today who wheedle, cajole or more often coerce the majority are more right. In any case, politics, like patriotism, is not enough. The reason is simple. "Politicians don't know the nature of reality. If they did, they would not be politicians. ... They act in ways that would be appropriate if such a world as they think they live in really existed. But, unfortunately, it does not exist except in their imagination. Hence nothing that they do is appropriate to the real world. And all their actions are actions of lunatics, and all, as history is there to demonstrate, are more or less disastrous."[15] In *Warriors of God* Walter Nigg concludes what is fairly obvious: "To expect any solution from statesmen is vain. They cannot give what they do not possess."[16].

The human mind has a thirst for explanation. Nature seems to satisfy that thirst. The thirst after righteousness is also part of the human psyche. As C. S. Lewis says, "If I find in myself a desire which no experience in this world can satisfy, the most probable explanation is that I was made for another world. If none of my earthly pleasures satisfy it, that does not prove the universe is a fraud. Probably earthly pleasures were never *meant* to satisfy it, but only to arouse it, to suggest the real thing."[17] The mystics are, as ever, interested in "the real thing." Now the human mind is so constituted that an explanation in terms of identity seems inherently plausible to it. To the scientist or the scientific view the entity called matter reveals itself as patterns of atom, or energy, or atomic energy, in some ways independent of time and space. This is the basic irreducible unity from which all diversities arise and to which they, in the end, return. The mystic cosmology has no quarrel with all this. The big difference comes in from the fact that whereas the scientist begins, as he must, from the bottom up, the mystic does it in the reverse, from top down. "As there, so here." In a characteristic image the *Veda* compares cosmic existence to a tree with "roots above." The principles are above and beyond fact, or are a different kind of facts, if you like. So while the ultimate to which science refers everything back is ultimate of Matter or Energy, the ultimate the mystic refers back to is a spiritual Absolute, absolutely Conscious and Self-Existent. There must be something in the human mind, or some modification of the mind, to which all this corresponds. The mystics believe that modification to be both actual and possible, in fact this is the next higher development of man, in which the opposition of physics and metaphysics might be healed. As to the difference in outlook and the results that follow, it will be enough to say, for the present, that this ancient conflict is not likely to be solved by logic arguing on the data of our ordinary physical existence. The solution can come only by an extension of our field of consciousness or by an unhoped-for increase in our instruments of knowledge. This, as we have seen, is part of the mystic faith and, more than that, mystic experience.

This is not to deny the validity of science within its own field. For, "whether the intellect is a help or a hindrance depends upon the person and upon the way in which it is used. . . . Any part of the being that keeps to its proper place and plays its appointed role is helpful; but directly it steps beyond its sphere it becomes twisted and perverted and therefore false."[18] Our own hypothesis is that in order to cover all the facts of existence—all, and not merely some of them—including the realm of values, we have to admit a hierarchy of the real. Otherwise in our eagerness to assert we are bound to deny one in order to affirm the other. And this is what has happened. The Materialist Denial and the Refusal of the Ascetic are equally one-sided, two sides of the same shield. As Whitehead has pointed out, "Some of the major disasters of mankind have been produced by the narrowness of men with a good methodology."[19] Eddington was even more specific: "There are certain states of awareness," he said, "mystical states, in consciousness that have at least equal significance with those which are called sensations."[20] Or as Rufus Jones puts it, "The mystics of Christian history present as solid a front of reliable testimony in their field as is the case with the testimony of science in its field through the time-belt."[21] Not the "mystics of Christian history alone," that is the only slight change one would like to make in that statement. The solid front includes all mystical traditions.

So it is that we can and must say that the scientific picture of the world is unreal and distorted, because limited to the quantitative. In *The Crisis of Our Age* Sorokin quotes a young scientist and his confession of faith: "Science," the young man says, "is not concerned with reality. . . . It is not for us as scientists to worry about 'reality'." They have left the worrying to the rest of us. But is it quite true that scientists have rejected any concern over reality? Most of them have either suggested, affirmed, or taken for granted that the scientific picture of the world *is* a real picture, the only real picture. In *Ends and Means*, Aldous Huxley explained the phenomenon at length. The scientific picture of the world is what it is, said Huxley, because men of science combine an incompetence to deal with the purely qualitative aspects of reality with certain special mathematical competences in regard to the purely quantitative aspects of reality. "They have no right to claim that this product of incompetence and specialization is a complete picture of reality. As a matter of historical fact, however, this claim has been constantly made." With the usual disastrous results.

It is not so well-known how this "impoverished reality" of science is the parent of the philosophy of meaninglessness and that secret hopelessness from which more people suffer than are willing to admit it. Thomas Henry Huxley called it a "nightmare" conception of the world. The American philosopher, Perry, has referred, in *Present Conflict of Ideals*, to an "alien world." Mumford has spoken of the "abolition of man." Rufus Jones, whom we have quoted earlier, has this to say: "Most of our present-day philosophy ends in thinness and sterility because the creators and interpreters of it have been misled into the easy belief that all the issues of life can be handled by the same methods and the same categories that have worked with astonishing success in physical, chemical and biological laboratories."[22] The effect of such a short-sighted and pseudo-scientific approach to the problems of human living and social reform can be seen in the complete disregard of the human personality and all ethical considerations, a free charter to violent revolutions and all manner of dictatorships and brainwashing. From these consequences there is no escape, unless we can find a more total world-view than the one our sciences have to offer. It is the claim and service of mystical experience that it gives one "the meaning of the whole" as nothing else can. It alone makes the "alien world" our home. In the stirring words of the Quaker mystic: "We have conquered the outward world, and put it in our nets, but the explorers of it are not yet 'at home' in the universe. We have immensely improved the means of life, but we have somehow failed to discover to expand the *meaning and significance of life*. . . . We must explore the 'labyrinthine ways' of our own selves. We must knock at the doors which lie within. . . . We have had our 'Westward Ho', our 'Northward Ho', our 'Southward Ho', and 'Stratosphere Ho', but we now need a ringing call to 'Inward Ho'."[23] The mystics have been ringing the bell for ages.

This brings us to our final issue—social planning. Planning is all the rage these days. "The agonised individual conscience . . . is no longer fashionable," wrote Bennett. "The social conscience is now in vogue. . . . But one may raise the question whether they (social ends) are best served by being thus set in the foreground of the mind."[24] Our socialists know better, in fact know nothing else. In this the evidence of Professor Laski will be as good as any other. In one of his later books, *Faith, Reason and Civilization*, he writes, "our victory will be thrown away unless we devote it to great ends." But what are these "great ends" according to Laski? He does not keep us in the dark for long. "I do not think," he continues "that anyone can examine with care our contemporary situation without being continually reminded that we again require some faith that will revitalize the human mind." And he has no doubts whatever where that revitalizing faith is to be found—in the Soviet Republic. " Despite all its cost in blood and toil and suffering, the dream has brought unbreakable hope to one-sixth of the surface of the world. Of course, it is not as yet, the fulfilment of the dream. But no one can easily deny that there is in the inner ethos of the Russian Revolution the clue to the secret which each race of men has ever pursued and from which it derived the dynamic of a revitalised freedom."

The challenge of that "inner ethos" need not be denied. It is a challenge indeed, in a sense other than Laski meant. But in terms of the ends that the mystics have put forward, the Russian Revolution might look like a heresy, a symptom rather than a remedy. In retrospect the brutal strategies of an unspiritualized soviet may turn out to be a consummation devoutly to be avoided, a red rather than a green signal. And, unlike Laski, one cannot afford to overlook the "cost in blood and toil and suffering" visited on others by the party machinery. Here is what another economist, with a mind maybe finer than Laski's, says about economic reconstruction: "The day is not far off when the economic problem will take the back seat where it belongs, and the arena of the heart and head will be occupied or re-occupied by our real problems—the problems of life and relations, of creation and behavior, and religion."[25] The men of science, economics and politics might feel disturbed by the way things are going, but by themselves, in terms of their special disciplines, they are unable to bring about any permanent solution of our persistent problems. They can tinker, they cannot transform. The "difficult alchemy, the transformation of men" is known only to the mystics and contemplatives and none else.[26] They alone have the right knowledge and make the right effort. They know, more than others do, that "only a total spiritual direction given to the whole of life and whole of nature can alone lift humanity beyond itself." Whether there will ever be a sufficiently receptive group that will work out the implications of such a profound change in human affairs is quite another question. However, it is significant, as Underhill has pointed out, "that many of these experiences are reported to us from periods of war and distress: that the stronger the forces of destruction appeared, the more intense grew the spiritual vision which opposed them. We learn from these records that the mystical consciousness has the power of lifting those who possess it to a plane of reality which no struggle, no cruelty, can disturb. . . . Rather it gives them a renewed vitality."[27] This gives us hope and one will not be surprised to find an echo, in modern terms, to St. Augustine's cry: My life shall be a real life, being wholly full of Thee. For even the modern man has had occasional glimpses of this truth, of the whole man, glimpses that are soon lost in the humanistic cloud. But a glimpse is not enough, what we need is an organized intuition, a steady lightning as the Veda puts it. How otherwise are we to welcome the Dawn of God, the dawn of "human history" of which the Ancients had seen the far-off promise? We must set all our resources to fulfill this pledge and promise. Or go under. In the midst of our modern anarchy, all the fear and trembling, the confusions of the twilight, as Sorokin has called it, the voice of the mystic, "a man the sciences have never known", rings out with clear confidence. As then, so now:

> The voice of one crying in the wilderness:
> Prepare the way of the Lord,
> Make his path straight.

As St. Paul said, "Now is the day of salvation." Or, at the risk of heresy, Eckhart: "It (mystical union) ranks so high that it communes with God face to face as He is. . . . (It) is unconscious of yesterday or the day before and of tomorrow and the day after, for in eternity there is no yesterday nor any tomorrow but only NOW." So now we must learn to discern and follow the mystic voice. It speaks to you and for you. "The land`which they see and which they report to us, is the land towards which humanity is going."[28] In the words of Tagore, the mystic is a bird of the dawn,[29] the forerunner of the soul-change to be. Pioneer of the spiritual world, in Time he waits for the

MYSTICS AS A FORCE FOR CHANGE

Eternal's hour, the substance of things hoped for. Or, as William Blake has it:

> I give you the end of a golden string,
>   Only wind it into a ball;
> It will lead you in at Heaven's gate—
>   Built in Jerusalem's wall.

Only wind it into a ball.

IV

The Doctrine
of the Mystics

Yet a system, a doctrine there is . . .

OBVIOUSLY the doctrine of the mystics is not the most important thing about them. Hocking says, rightly, "Mysticism then, we shall not define by its doctrines." Yet the mistake, or confusion, has been frequently made. Bertrand Russell revealed a characteristic turn of mind and, on this matter, a common attitude when he said: "The mystic insight begins with the sense of mystery unveiled, of a hidden wisdom now suddenly become certain beyond the possibility of a doubt. The sense of certainty and revelation comes earlier than any definite belief. The definite beliefs at which mystics arrive are a result of reflection upon the inarticulate experiences gained in moments of insight." But all who know know that "the moments of insight" are more veridical than the "reflections" that follow, that the mystical way of living is more central than speculative mysticism. Pascal's experience was that of

God of Abraham, God of Isaac, God of Jacob,
Not of the philosophers and the learned.

But the error, or distinction has the *imprimatur* of "the learned", viz., *Encyclopaedia of Religion and Ethics*. It restricts the word "mysticism" "as designating the historic doctrine of the relationship and potential union of the human soul with the Ultimate Reality and to use the world 'mystical experience' for direct intercourse with God." The general view has been stated by Butler: "Of course there may be a philosophy of mysticism...but mysticism as such has nothing to say to philosophy...[it] is not a philosophy, it is an experience."[1] The doctrine, mostly derivative and secondary, is in the nature of deductions and inferences, rationalizations or mental translations, it points to as it is based upon the mystical experience. But these "reflections" are not the heart of the mystery.

In itself, the experience is held to be a fact. This the mystics have always held. It is also "ineffable", "beyond all expression". "Not by speech, not by thought, not by sight does one grasp Him. *He is:* by that word and not otherwise is He comprehended." Such is the classic Indian formula, echoed everywhere; by the Zen Masters, for instance. According to Bodhidharma, *satori* is "knowledge of the most adequate kind; only it cannot be expressed in words.". According to Tai-hui, "To talk about the unfathomable or mysterious is defiling." Such has been the general theory or attitude towards the mystery of the mystic experience or knowledge among the masters of those that know. The semantic difficulty, if not impossibility, is not unknown to such among the moderns who have had occasional, if not unexpected, brushes with the beyond. "Impossible to describe," wrote Bucke; "utterly beyond words," were the words Tennyson used; Symonds "could not find words to render it intelligible"; Koestler found "the experience meaningful though not in verbal terms". Our human vocabulary loses all its meanings, said Rufus Jones.

And yet doctrines form a familiar, if not an essential, feature of the mystic landscape. A complete blank between the empirical and transcendental consiciousness is not desirable. Some sort of relation or linkage there must be. There is a paradox here and throughout. As Stace puts it, "Some are content to call it inexpressible. Much nevertheless has been written about it."[2] Mystical theology in the west and spiritual philosophies in the east are part of the proof. Often "dogmatic" and nearly always paradoxical, the mystical statements carry a kind of *ipse dixit* and make dialogue difficult. The assumption of superior wisdom by uncommon, mysterious or dubious devices is apt to be resented. But the compelling force of its appeal and argument is among the best that the world has known. From Plotinus to Sri Aurobindo, it is true, "mystics themselves philosophize," with breathtaking subtlety. Though the severely practical Buddha forbade metaphysical debates or speculations, there is, as Dean Inge has said, "and must be a philosophy of mysticism...[it] has indeed been worked out by several thinkers of genius."[3] In Shankara and Eckhart, for instance, we have the "almost unbelievable spectacle" of two of the strictest scholastics laboring hard and with unwonted brilliance over a non-rational, inconceivable Godhead. As Rudolf Otto pointed out, "Nowhere does doctrine play a greater part than with these two mystics."[4] And yet both of them knew "*Atman* is not capable of proof nor does it need any", and believed: "The most beautiful thing which man can say of God is that, knowing His inner riches he becomes silent. Therefore prate not of God." "He, or It, is *svasiddha,* self-proven, that is axiomatic, the knowledge is an incommunicable science."[5]

Then why do they themselves "prate", or attempt the impossible and the unnecessary? Because it is not without its use and the difficulty surrounding the statement of doctrine is not deliberate. Apparently the doctrine, or statement of doctrine, is trying to do something that has little chance of success, and yet they do it. The statements and generalizations refer to a level of cognition or experience, where, to believe them, opposites are reconciled and logic as we know it ceases to function, at least ceases to dominate discourse. And since the experience carries with it its own authority the logical difficulty must be faced, in any case it cannot be used against the original experience superseding normal logic. In other words, the experience of the mystic is not discursive but intuitive, to use a word highly charged with emotional overtones and the sight of which throws many scientists into dismay and disagreement. But in most cases the doctrine, whatever it is, does attempt a kind of discourse, for the need to relate the trans-logical—"Before Whom, or Which, words recoil"—with our normal awareness of the world and its processes remains. To our ordinary ways of thinking and being every such attempt smacks of challenge and a kind of violence, it is full of contradictions which the intellect is unable either to accept or endorse. About the paradoxical nature of these statements, which we have already mentioned, it is, by the way, taken for granted that they *are* like that. All who have been through the mystic woods and know the rules of the game know that paradox—"Vacuum plenum," as someone describes this—is the foundation and structure of all mysticism. One might even say that it is paradoxical because it is true. In this matter modern aesthetics could easily take a lesson or two from the old wisdom. Take this from the well-known statment in the *Isha Upanishad*: "That One, the Self, though never stirring, is swifter than thought....Though standing still, it overtakes those who are running....It stirs and it stirs not." Or Lao-tse, the master of the masters of paradox:

The Way is like an empty vessel
That may yet be drawn from
Without ever needing to be filled.
It is bottomless: the very progenitor of all things
    in the world...
It is like a deep pool that never dries.
I do not know whose child it could be.
It looks as if it were prior to God.

Or this, which closes most invocations in India: "Full is That. Full is This. Fullness is drawn from the Full. Take Fullness from the Full; it remains always Full." It is plain that such "Fullness" is fully beyond most of us most of the time. To the strict logical mind it is another name for foolishness. No wonder Bertrand Russell could not swallow the bait, "the peculiar logic of mysticism which discounts the two fundamental laws of natural logic, the law of contradiction and excluded middle."

Apparently the doctrine, and the experience supporting it, ante-date philosophy and mathematics, and may one day out-date these too. It is metaphysical and based on a knowledge by identity. In some ways, it is simplicity itself. "The Ground of God and the Ground of the Soul are one and the same," says Eckhart. Again, from the same authority, "The intuitive, higher knowledge is timeless and spaceless, without any here and now."[6] This is not merely an ancient mystery and possession. Many modern voices echo it. It may come of itself or through effort, that is not so important at the moment. To quote a familiar passage from Tennyson's *Memoirs*: "A kind of waking trance I have frequently had, quite up from my boyhood, when I have been alone. This has generally come upon me through repeating my own name two or three times to myself silently, till all at once, as it were out of the intensity of the consciousness of individuality, the individuality itself seemed to dissolve and fade away into boundless being; and this is not a confused state, but the clearest of the clearest, the surest of the surest, the weirdest of the weirdest, utterly beyond words, where death was an almost laughable impossibility, the loss of personality (if so it were) seeming no extinction but the only true life." This is a persistent note. Its justification is based on what has been described as a "supreme identity."[7] Brevity is the soul of this identity and wisdom, and Poincaré who insisted on the elegance of theories ought to have been delighted with this, same and simple, always. *Thou art That*, is a famous Indian formulation. Or, in Christianity, *I and my Father are one.* All is in that, all follows from that.

Or if we prefer modern, that is abstract, terminology, the doctrine or experience in question is "an ultimate non-sensuous unity in all things." Or, to use Northrop's equally polysyllabic phrase, it is "an undifferentiated aesthetic continuum."

The only way to get out of the "undifferentiated" difficulty of such formulations would be, as we have already suggested, to admit degrees of knowledge, a higher and a lower knowledge, known to all ancient systems and mystics the world over, the higher shading off into grace, while the lower is confined to the world of naturalistic operations. "The soul has something within it," writes Eckhart, "a spark of supersensual knowledge that is never quenched. But then there is also another knowledge in our souls, which is turned towards outward object: namely, knowledge of the senses and understanding: this hides that other knowledge from us." Obviously both kinds are needed, as the *Isha Upanishad* tells us, both the knowledge of world and knowledge of self. Even Bertrand Russell, whose views on mysticism are often partisan and superficial, had noted: "The greatest men who have been philosophers have felt the need both of science and of mysticism...and (the union of the two) the highest eminence...possible to achieve in the world of thought." That would involve, as Plotinus might say, "another way of seeing which everyone has but few use." The mystics are among the few that do, and "the wisdom of this world is foolishness with God" and the mystics. The objection that mysticism is a religion for the few has perhaps to be faced. But, it must also be admitted, as some of the examples have shown, that "the minor forms of mysticism are shared by a large number of people and are quite possible, though latent, for a great many more."[8]

Another distinction of the doctrine, which sets it apart from philosophy of the academic and scientific variety, is that it is a science of the soul and salvation, *muktir upāya, mokṣaśāstra*. What must I do to be saved? Above all you must know. You are saved through knowledge. It is a typical error to say, as one of its eminent exponents has done, that "Mysticism is in essence little more than a certain intensity and depth of feeling in regard to what is believed about the universe." Not a "little more" but a lot more and lot different. It is indeed a form of pure perception, through doors that have been first cleansed through discipline, devotion and detachment. "Seeing Him alone, one transcends death; there is no other way," says the *Swetaswatara Upanishad*, of things not merely felt but known. Similarly the *Book of Common Prayer* says: "God, in knowledge of whom standeth our eternal life." The seer of the *Mundaka Upanishad* was not expressing a mere feeling but a knowledge, the knowledge by identity, as we have called it before. "He who knows Brahman becomes Brahman. He passes beyond all sorrow...Freed from the fetters of Ignorance he becomes Immortal."

Even the Buddha, who scrupulously avoided the *O Altitudo!* speaks in the same vein. What is the greatest sin? he asks. The answer is, Stupidity. And the way out is through knowledge, not feeling. Whether the Buddha was a mystic or not, his teaching had but one savor, salvation.

Desire, [tanhā], Ignorance [avidyā], or Original Sin, it comes to the same thing. "That which will not make me (free and) immortal, what shall I do with that?" That ancient cry, wrung out of a woman's heart (the soul is feminine), first heard in the forest retreats of India, still rings, and will continue to do so as long as men suffer from homesickness for the country of the soul. The doctrine of the mystics may be compared to a road map, of the Way of Return, ultā path. As Bergson said, it is a remounting of the natural slope of our minds. But it is no part of a conducted tour. Each must explore the way— alone. It is the flight of the alone to the Alone, the plunge into naked Nothingness. This loneliness is part of the very process of learning. According to Madame Montessori: "The child who has never learned to act alone, to direct his own actions, to govern his own will, grows into an adult who is easily led and must always lean upon other." Such adults are easy victims of the monstrous creed of mass culture and the proliferating persuaders of the advertisement agencies.

Mystical philosophy, which tries to describe the different stations of this journey or union, is not always or altogether a scholastic hairsplitting, the product of overheated, lazy brains. It is true it has a tendency to degenerate into a game, of futile subtleties and dogmatics, odium theologicum, into attempts to find out how many angels could be balanced on a pinpoint, which, by the way, is a less dangerous way of passing one's time than releasing all the chained devils of destruction from a single invisible atom out of a uranium pile. But the same divine doctor, who had been looking for angels on pinpoints, after he had been smitten by a genuine mystical experience, preferred silence and gave up theology. "I have seen that which makes all that I have written and taught look small to me. My writing days are over," said St. Thomas Aquinas. This is an excellent illustration of both the need of theology and its limitation. Doctrine, theology, metaphysics are like a ladder or a system of scaffolding. They are a help and we do not have to kick them after we have reached the heights, for we might need them again on our way back. Never is the ladder or scaffolding an end, it is always a means, which many need. And while all men may not need it in the same measure, as a matter of convenience most do.

The doctrine of the mystics implies, as we have said before, levels of reality, mind and consciousness, "through many linking stages". Man, said Eucken, is the meeting-ground of various stages of Reality, Or, as the French psychologist, Binet, once put it: "There would be some naivety in holding that this consciousness which is personal to us and in which we usually remain is the only one existing in us."[9] What Bucke tried to popularize as "cosmic consciousness" has been always known and accepted by mystics in some form or other. Here is a somewhat modern statement of the ancient reality, as seen by a mystic of our own times, Sri Aurobindo:

"Matter expresses itself eventualy as a formulation of some unknown Force. Life, too, that yet unfathomed mystery, begins to reveal itself as an obscure energy of sensibility imprisoned in its material formulation; and when the dividing ignorance is cured which gives us the sense of a gulf between Life and Matter, it is difficult to suppose that Mind, Life and Matter will be found to be anything else than one Energy triply formulated, the triple world of the Vedic seers. Nor will the conception then be able to endure of a brute material Force as the mother of Mind. The Energy that creates the world can be nothing else than a Will, and Will is only conscousness applying itself to a work and a result.

"What is that work and result, if not a self-involution of Consciousness in form and a self-evolution out of form so as to actualise some mightly possibility in the universe which it has created? And what is its will in Man if not a will to unending Life, to unbounded Knowlege, to unfettered Power? Science itself begins to dream of the physical conquest of death, expresses an insatiable thirst for knowledge, is working out something like a terrestrial omnipotence for humanity. Space and Time are contracting to the vanishing-point in its works, and it strives in a hundred ways to make the master of circumstance and so lighten the fetters of causality. The idea of limit, of the impossible begins to grow a little shadowy and it appears instead that whatever man constantly wills, he must in the end be able to do; for the consciousness in the race eventually finds the means....It is this vast cosmic impulse which the modern world, without quite knowing its own aim, yet serves in all its activities and labours subconsciously to fulfil."[10]

Such a liberal understanding, or inner view, of cosmic processes and purposes, shows mysticism itself to be a science as well as a way of life. Josiah Royce always insisted that the mystics were "the only thoroughgoing empiricists in the history of philosophy." After examining the evidence impartially Marquette reached the conclusion: "In the very name of experimental science, this collective testimony (of the mystics all over the world and in every age) cannot be brushed aside, and must be reckoned with in any serious attempt to understand human nature and its possibilities."[11] As an experimental science it has a technique or discipline of its own, *methodus mystica*, yoga; *dhyāna*, orison, contemplation, call it what you will. In *The Meaning of God in Human Experience* Hocking has described mysticism as an "experimental wisdom", having its own methods and its own audacious intention of meeting deity face to face. "The experimental perception of God's Presence and Being" has always been part of the mystic claim and rationale. It is true, however, that where the scholastics have triumphed, "mystical theology tended more and more to become a science of contemplation rather than a religious experience."

Spontaneous or uncontrollable or part of a schedule, techniques for inducing mystical states—including the use of drugs, now once again alarmingly on the increase —have been known from the earliest times. Among genuine mystics there is an agreement that the path is austere and should avoid, as far as possible, any dependence on external aids. Truths occult exist not for ignorant and drugged minds. Only the pure in heart shall see God or the Truth that makes one free. Hence the insistence, in nearly all schools of mysticism, on detachment and devotion, choice and contemplation. These have been among well-tested psychological disciplines, which our present-day secularized, advertisement-boozed minds have a hard time in accepting.

Another fact about the mystic discipline and doctrine which the modern mind shies at is the mystery in which the whole thing seems to be shrouded. There is a feeling that this knowledge is for the few, the initiates. It sounds rather undemocratic. Why secrecy? they ask. The simplest answer is "Try and you will know." The knowledge is the result of a special kind of concentrating of all one's energies. It calls for laboratory conditions necessary for any prolonged research. It is not secret in the sense that it has never been told. It would not be understood even if told—unless one first verified it within the silence of the spirit, alone. The secrecy is due to the nature of the truth and out of respect for the personality of the seeker. It would cease to be a truth if it could be mass-produced and consumed by a crowd. There is no short cut to it nor can fools be trusted with it. The masters are not inhuman but wise.

But in spite of its universal core the mystical experience as well as the mystical doctrine has shown the greatest diversity. It is not monolithic or monotonous. As Rudolf Otto has said, in spite of much formal agreement, mystic experience is capable of great diversity. Theistic, atheistic, ethical, supra-ethical, pantheistic, transcendental, there are many variations, understandably. Because the truth that we are dealing with is a truth of the Infinite, at once one and many. This is a simple fact of experience and not a deliberate mystification.

But if mystical experience and doctrines have assumed many shapes, spoken with many voices, "the resemblances are far more striking—the differences are superficial."[12] Basically, the Way is one. As Dorothy Phillipps has pointed out: "Whatever the approach, and however complicated the philosophical or theological superstructures erected upon it, the essentials of the Way whereby Reality becomes transformingly effective in the individual life were found to be identical and universal."[13] Rudolf Otto somewhere calls this a "polar identity". As Aldous Huxley has repeatedly said, "At all times and in all places, the free have spoken with only one voice." This does not mean that dissident voices are not there; they are, both noisy and frequent, but the very fact proves that they do not belong, among the knowers of truth, but among those that know little or nothing.

Whatever minor differences there might be in the doctrine of the mystics, it always adds up to a total revaluation of our values, the only one worth having. It alone has a right to be, for it alone changes the foundation, the very texture of our consciousness, the ground or door of perception. Mysticism stands for the greatest revolution in human condition. It alone can counterbalance "this death of purpose"[14] which infects the modern world through and through. At the end of his life, the utopian H. G. Wells wrote that "the more he weighed the realities before him, the less he was able to detect any convergence whatever."[15] It is needless to point out that mysticism was not among the Wellsian "realities". Mysticism lacks and usually rejects the compulsive instruments of social, political and religious organizations and is better thus. It proposes the only kind of change that really matters. It asks men to change themselves and their ways. It is not that the doctrine by itself, not even the experience by itself, will open the door and do everything. No, all these are but counters, or like science, pointer readings, they point towards Reality, towards the More that we must be. Sometimes pessimistic on the outside, mysticism is our only hope.

There is, in fact, no other aim or theory of life that gives human life such dignity as the mystical. It points to "a living God and a personal self capable of communing with Him." Even where it is not theistic, the results are surprisingly alike, at least noble, better than what the non-mystical ever achieve or are capable of achieving. At least it defies or breaks the materialist mold and that is a great release. As Rhine has suggested: "It is the bearing of *psi* on an understanding of the nature of the human being...a faint flutter of encouragement to offset the depressing conception of man that is inherent in the atmosphere of this mechanistic age."[16] It points to a source of secret identity or immortality, an inheritance to which, at some stage or other, something in man responds. Perhaps the greatest value of the theory or doctrine is that it brings back meaning to life, the meaning of the Whole. Without being unduly anthropocentric, we whose mind is now at the end of its tether ought to know what it means. Mysticism is inherently ontological, the only "ism" that has a right to be so. In this view "All life is only a lavish and manifold opportunity given us to discover, realise and express the Divine." (The accent is on "all".) No philosophy of life can hold a candle to that, certainly not our popular prophets of doom and latter-day existentialists, saints and satanists alike. The one way to cure and confront them is to posit the reality of mystical insight, an insight into the Essence as a part of man's increasing and inevitable experience of life and himself, if only he will cooperate with the emerging Truth. The doctrine of the mystics—and, we repeat, the mystical experience—are the only antidote to all the decadence and the diseases of civilization that seem to swamp us on all sides. To the "meaningless absurdity of life" which once darkened the mind of Tolstoy no less than that of many others, before and after, more and less known, there is but one answer —an experiential answer, that of the mystics, the saints and the seers. They have weathered the storm, gone through the veriest hell, not for a season of adolescent outing but with all the sober certainty of a mature encounter with the principle of evil, and yet stand firm, on the unassailable grounds of Being, *Sat, Istigkeit.* ("My mind in the flash of a trembling glance came to Absolute Being—That Which Is —and other than Which Nothing Is.") It is a mariner's compass in man's long journey through time and the "waters" of life. Mysticism will not so much give us any worldly truth or direction (e.g., "How To Win Friends and Influence People") but "the whole working essence," "the meaning of the whole." It needs no other justification.

As a rule the mystical doctrine has been presented in metaphorical or symbolical terms. Jesus spoke through parables. "In parables spake he unto them....Unto you it is given to know the mystery of the Kingdom of God." Here, drawing upon Sri Aurobindo, we present, in outline, one version of the doctrine, from the archetypal poetry of the Vedas, which has the advantage that it also explains itself:

"Mystics...had an enormous influence on...early civilizations; there was indeed almost everywhere an age of the Mysteries in which men of a deeper knowledge and self-knowledge established their practices, significant rites, symbols, secret lore within or on the border of the more primitive exterior religions. This took different forms in different countries; in Greece there were the Orphic and Eleusinean Mysteries, in Egypt and Chaldea the priests and their occult lore and magic, in Persia the *Magi*, in India the *Rishis*. The preoccupation of the Mystics was with self-knowledge and a profounder world-knowledge; they found out that in man there was a deeper self and inner being behind the surface of the outward physical man, which it was his highest business to discover and know. 'Know Thyself' was their great precept, just as in India to know the Self, the *Atman* became the great spiritual need, the highest thing for the human being. They found also a Truth, a Reality behind the outward aspects of the universe and to discover, follow, realize this Truth was their great aspiration. They discovered secrets and powers of Nature which are not those of the physical world and physical things but which could bring occult mastery over the physical world and physical things and to systematize this occult knowledge and power was also one of their preoccupations. But all this could only be safely done by a difficult and careful training, discipline, purification of the nature; it could not be done by the ordinary man. If men entered into these things without a severe test and training it would be dangerous to themselves and others; this knowledge, these powers could be misused, misinterpreted, turned from truth to falsehood, from good to evil. A strict secrecy was therefore maintained, the knowledge handed down behind a veil from master to disciple. A veil of symbols was created behind which these mysteries could shelter,. formulas of speech also which could be understood by the initiated but were either not known by others or were taken by them in outward sense which carefully covered their true meaning and secret. This was the substance of Mysticism everywhere."

Such ideas do not easily fit into the prevailing picture of social growth and progress from a primitive past. To admit an intuitive element in our ancestors is like upsetting the apple cart of the theory of a unilinear evolution and the universe. "The ancient idea about the Veda could not fit into this picture; it was regarded as rather a part of ancient superstitious ideas and a primitive error. But we can now form a more accurate idea of the development of the race. The ancient, more primitive civilizations held in themselves the elements of the later growth but their early wise men were not scientists and philosophers or men of high intellectual reason but mystics and even mystery-men, occultists, religious seekers; they were seekers after a veiled truth behind things and not of an outward knowledge. The scientists and philosophers came afterwards; they were preceded by the mystics and, often, like Plato and Pythagoras, were to some extent mystics themselves or drew many of their ideas from the mystics. In India philosophy grew out of the seeking of the mystics and retained and developed their spiritual aims and kept something of their methods in later Indian spiritual discipline and Yoga."

Through the symbols of discipline and the high training of will the seeker was moved towards a vision of "a Truth deeper and higher than the truth of outward existence, a Light greater and higher than the light of human understanding which comes by revelation and inspiration, an immortality towards which the soul has to rise. We have to find our way to that, to get into touch with this Truth and Immortality,...to be born into the Truth, to grow into it, to ascend in spirit into the world of Truth and to live in it. To do so is to unite ourselves with the Godhead and to pass from mortality into immortality." This is the first and the central teaching of the Vedic mystics. The Platonists, developing their doctrine from the early mystics, held that we live in relation to two worlds,—a world of higher truth which might be called the spiritual world and that in which we live, the world of the embodied soul which is derived from the higher but also degraded from it into an inferior truth and inferior consciousness. The Vedic mystics held this doctrine in a more concrete and pragmatic form, for they had the experience of these two worlds. There is the inferior truth here of this world mixed as it is with much falsehood and error, and there is a world or home of Truth, the Right, the Vast....There are many worlds between up to the triple heavens and their lights but this is the world of the highest Light—the world of the Sun of Truth or the Great Heaven. We have to find the path to this Great Heaven, the path of Truth, or as it is sometimes called the way of the gods. This is the second mystic truth. The third is that our life is a battle between the powers of Light and Truth, the Gods who are Immortals and the powers of Darkness. ...We have to invoke the Gods by the inner sacrifice... Our sacrifice is a journey, a pilgrimage and a battle,—a travel towards the Gods and we also make the journey with Agni, the inner Flame, as our pathfinder and leader. Our human things are raised up by the mystic Fire into the immortal being, into the Great Heaven, and the things divine come down into us....Finally, as the summit of the teaching of the Vedic mystics comes the secret of one Reality[17]...and one bliss to which we must rise."

"Our earth shaped out of the dark inconscient ocean of existence lifts its high formations and ascending peaks heavenward; heaven of mind has its own formations, clouds that give out lightnings and their waters of life; the streams of the clarity and the honey ascend out of the subconscient ocean below and seek the superconscient ocean above; and from above that ocean sends downward its rivers of the light and truth and bliss even into our physical being. Thus in images of physical Nature the Vedic poets sing the hymn of our spiritual ascension.

"That ascension has already been effected by the Ancients, the human forefathers, and the spirit of these great Ancestors still assist their offspring....The seven sages are waiting still and always, ready to chant the word, to rend the cavern, to find the lost herds, to recover the hidden Sun....The soul is a battlefield,...a world full of beings, a kingdom in which armies clash to help or hinder a supreme conquest, a house where the gods are our guests and which the demons strive to possess....Every shining godward Thought that arises from the secret abysses of the heart is a priest and a creator."[18]

In other words, the soul of man is a seat of sacrifice, a diving board into the seas of superconscience. What we do with it is the measure of what we have done with life and its possibilities. The choice is always ours. As Lecomte du Noüy has said: "Until man appeared, evolution strove only, from an observer's point of view, to manufacture an organ....Man continues to play his part but wants to comprehend the play....Instead of depending as formerly on the slow action of the biological laws and of chance, natural selection now depends on conscience...based on freedom which becomes in each of us the means put at our disposal to advance. According to the degree of evolution we have reached we will choose to progress or regress."[19]

Such, in brief, is the teaching of the mystics, or some of it. There can be no doubt that they have chosen, and as to what they have chosen. Whether and how far their example will inspire others each man must answer for himself. For always, and for a long time, the ascent, the awakening, the encounter, the sacrifice, is individual. Mass or forced conversion is not the mystic way. You alone are free and responsible, free to be free. The mystical claim, of an "experimental science", stands or falls by its psychology, primarily a psychology of the individual, and his destiny. To this we now turn.

V

The Role
of the Individual

What is man that thou art mindful of him?

THE mystics do not make the mistake of treating man as the measure of things. But, in their own way, they give him an even wider value, an unlimited liability and destiny such as no other view of life can or does. To time's fools they hold up a wisdom beyond time. The value of such an undertaking will be obvious from the findings of two modern psychologists. "Since insight is our greatest need," they write, "the greatest task psychology faces today is the task of discovering new ways of satisfying that need—not only of bringing more insight to more people, but of finding why it is the simple process of living seems to diminish rather than increase it."[1] We who live in such a world of diminishing return have need of this. Among mystics there is general agreement that life in a human body provides uniquely good opportunities for achieving salvation or deliverance. It is at once man's duty and right. In the Upanishads the suggestion is often met with

63

that a man who leaves the world—gentle euphemism for death—without first knowing *Brahman* has missed his chance, indeed has missed everything, that for which he had been born. In the words of a modern mystic: "Therefore man's importance in the world is that he gives to life that development of consciousness in which its transfiguration by a perfect self-discovery becomes possible." What a responsibility!

Extremes of world-negation apart, most mature forms of mysticism hold out the promise of a conscious evolution, an enlargement of interests and relations, both for the individual and the group. In the mystical view of life "The ascent to the divine Life is the human journey, the work of Works, the acceptable Sacrifice. This alone is man's real business in the world and the justification of his existence, without which he would be only an insect crawling among other ephemeral insects on a speck of surface mud and water which has managed to form itself amid the appalling immensities of the physical universe."[3]

For this to be real the individual is necessary, to justify the ways of God or divine becoming. History without Incarnation is "bunk". Independently, He exists in Himself, but through the individual He manifests himself in relation. That, to put the matter a little metaphysically, is the justification of the individual, his "real business" here, even if the *Wall Street Journal* has not heard of it.

But such a promise, or premise, is based upon a psychological view of things, very different from the current ones. The simplest way to describe this would be to call it a transcendental psychology, only one must be prepared to qualify it and others perhaps to accept the qualification. The mystic is not necessarily a perfect human being. Very often he is not. But, always, if he is a mystic at all, he admits a further becoming of man, to become what he is, to use Nietzsche's dark phrase. The mystic's sense of life and adventure of mind strains upward, "beyond all present maps." The world of the senses, of material facts and goals of life is never enough for him. In all this he feels the sense of something missing. Keenly aware of his limitations, death, desire and incapacity impel him to seek for their opposites, to dream of release, desirelessness and victory. He feels differently and, when the eyes have been opened, knows better. Metaphysically sound, the mystic psychology is based on experiment and verification, just like any other. It is, as we have maintained throughout, a science; only its methods, field and basic assumptions differ, sometimes radically, from the popular versions. Simply put, in the mystic view man appears as a meeting-place of various levels of reality. The mystic's main interest lies in effecting a transition from the lower to the higher, and, after the transition has been secured, a transformation of the lower in terms of the higher. Word became Flesh, so that Flesh might become Word.

> A mutual debt binds man to the Supreme:
> His nature we must put on as he put ours;
> We are sons of God and must be even as he:
> His human portion, we must grow divine.
> Our life is a paradox with God for key.

Man as he is, is a mid-term, he never is but always to be blest. This shows what many dislike and suspect about the mystical business, that the psychology is intuitive, the psychology of beatitude and deification. "This is the life of the gods and godlike and blessed men—a liberation from the alien that besets us here," was Plotinus's phrase for this state. A defense of the intuitive position would be quite easy. As Allport has pointed out: "William James, for example, invoked the hypothesis of a subliminal connection between the individual mind and a universal mind. The island of individual consciousness, to use his analogy, rests ultimately upon the limitless ocean floor from which it draws its composition and support. The theory that the individual mind is merely a fragment of a universal mind is common in many religions as diverse in type as Hinduism and Christian Science. To some extent this theory seems to be present in nearly every religion. Its merit, as James himself clearly saw, is metaphysical rather than psychological. It provides a possible channel for the rush of divine consciousness into the individual mind."[4] And that is what we have earlier called the promise of transcendental psychology. In the simple words of Swami Vivekananda, who may be taken to speak for the Indian tradition and standpoint: "There is a continuity of mind, as the yogis call it. The mind is universal. Your mind, my mind, all these little minds, are fragments of the universal mind, little waves in the ocean; and on account of this continuity we can convey our thoughts directly to one another."[5] As regards intuition, if we will but look closely, "In each stage of Matter, in each stage of Life, the Intuition assumes a working proper to that stage and acts from behind the veil supporting and enforcing the immediate necessities of the creative Force. There is an Intuition in matter which holds the action of the material world from the electron to the sun and planets and their contents. There is an intuition in Life which similarly supports and guides the play and development of Life in Matter till it is ready for the mental evolution of which man is the vehicle. In man also the creation follows the same upward process,—the Intuition within develops according to the stage he has reached in his progress. Even the precise intellect of the scientist, who is inclined to deny the separate existence or the superiority of Intuition, yet cannot really move forward unless there is behind him a mental Intuition, which enables him to take a forward step or to devine what has to be done. Intuition therefore is present at the beginning of things and in their middle as well as at their consummation."[6] If one is still skeptical and should ask for the reason why, here is the reason: "It is a sound rule inherent in the very constitution of universal existence that where there are truths attainable by the reason there must be somewhere in the organism possessed of that reason a means of arriving at or verifying them by experience. The one means we have left in our mentality is an extension of that form of knowledge by identity which gives us the awareness of our existence. It is really upon a self-awareness more or less conscient, more or less present to our conception that our knowledge of the contents of our self is based. Or to put it in a more general formula, the knowledge of the contents is contained in the knowledge of the continent. If then we can extend our faculty of mental self-awareness to awareness of the Self beyond and outside us (*Atman* or *Brahman* of the *Upanishads*), we may become possessors in experience of the truths which form the contents of the *Atman* or *Brahman*. It is on this possibility that Indian *Vedanta* has based itself. It has sought through the knowledge of the Self the knowledge of the universe."[7] In the simpler style of Lao-tse, "Without going out of doors, you may know the whole world." Or, as Plotinus has it, "Each being contains within itself the whole intelligible world. Therefore all is everywhere. Each is there all and all is in each." In the words of an early theologian: "It is necessary to know, in the first place, that the God, who is the fabricator of man, produced his form, his condition, and his whole essence, in the image and similitude of the world...And thus the Demiurges exhibited man by the artifice of a divine fabrication, in such a way, that, in a small body, we ight bestow the power and essence of all the elements, nature for this purpose bringing them together; and also, so that from the divine spirit, which descended from a celestial intellect to the support of the mortal body, he might prepare an abode for man, which, though fragile, *might be similar to the world....* So that the animal *which was made in imitation of the world* might be governed by an essence similarly divine."[8]

This is the mystic's point of departure, what he has sought and found and therefore cannot deny. So far as he is concerned there is nothing hypothetical about it, a knowledge "curiously self-consistent and often mutually explanatory." If the rest of the world were to disregard and disown, as has happened often, he would walk alone, the eternal outsider. But it is to the outsiders that the world has owed most, even if it has now and then forgotten to be grateful.

From what has been said it is easy to see that the psychology of the mystics is really a study and quest of consciousness or Self. The difficulty of the modern man is well described by Ouspensky. "Never in history," says Ouspensky, "has psychology stood at *so low a level* ... lost all touch with its *origin* and *meaning*...perhaps the *oldest science* and unfortunately, in its most essential features, a *forgotten science*, the science of his possible evolution."[9] It is, as we can see, a psychology of levels or dimensions, deeper than most "depth" psychologies. The fifth dimension, as Rosenkrantz says, is the liberating dimension.[10] In some ways this sounds esoteric. But this is true of all science. The laws of things are never on the surface. Only the mystics do not take the material alone to be the real. They go further without always faring worse. In support of their procedure they refer, just as much as the scientist does, to our powers of analysis, observation, and experiment. Also, they do not refuse to accept the material formula so much as refuse to accept it as final and the only one. The mystics speak of man the machine, but they also refer to that in man which is more than machine and capable of making him an agent or expression of freedom. They know, what nearly everyone some time or other suspects, that the individual is part of a larger Self. This knowledge, for it is really that, they are unwilling and unable to give up, to oblige those whose prejudices or lack of understanding keep them outside this liberalizing experience. But a little sympathy and open-mindedness is often enough to release the possibility. As a result of his experiments in extra-sensory perceptions William James had arrived at the following honest but unorthodox conclusions: "One conclusion was forced upon my mind and my impression of its truth has ever since remained unshaken. It is that our normal waking consciousness, rational consciousness, as we call it, is but one special type of consciousness, whilst all about it, parted from it by the filmiest of screens, there lie potential forms of consciousness entirely different. We may go through life without suspecting their existence; but apply the requisite stimulus, and at a touch they are there in all their completeness, definite types of mentality which probably somewhere have their field of application and adaptation. No account of the universe in its totality can be final which leaves these other forms of consciousness quite disregarded. How to regard them is the question—for they are so discontinuous with ordinary consciousness. Yet they may determine attitudes though they cannot furnish formulas, and open a region, though they may fail to give a map. At any rate, they forbid a premature closing of our accounts with reality."[11]

With all this the mystics would whole-heartedly agree. For whoever else—and that, unfortunately, includes nearly everybody—may have closed the account with reality, the mystic minority at least has kept its accounts open and straight, kept faith in "the seed of God in us". Only in keeping with the nature of their inquiry the technique has been different and necessarily more inward. In the course of his "Experimental Mysticism" Ouspensky discovered, "knowledge of the real world was possible, but, it became clearer and clearer to me during my experiments, it required a different approach and a different preparation." This approach and preparation has as much right to be considered scientific as any other inquiry into the secrets of nature and self, and what might be beyond both. In the words of Edward Carpenter, obviously based on his experiments or experience known to the eastern mystics from the dawn of history: "Of all the hard facts of life . . . I know of none more solid and fundamental than that if you inhibit thought (and persevere), you come at length to a region of consciousness below and behind thought and different from ordinary thought in its nature and character—a consciousness of quasi-universal quality, and a realization of an altogether vaster self than that to which we are accustomed. And since the ordinary consciousness with which we are concerned in ordinary life, is before all things founded on the little, local self, and is in fact self-consciousness in the little, local sense, it follows that to pass out of that is to die to the ordinary self and the ordinary world. It is to die in the ordinary sense, but in another sense it is to wake up and find that the I, one's real, most intimate self pervades the universe and all other beings—that the mountains and the sea and the stars are a part of one's body and that one's soul is in touch with the souls of all creatures. Yes, far closer than before. It is to be assured of an indestructible, immortal life and of a joy immense and inexpressible. . . . All life is changed. . . . For the ceaseless endeavor to realize this identity with the great Self, there is no substitute. No teaching, no theorizing, no philosophizing, no rules of conduct of life will take the place of actual experience. This is the Divine Yoga or union, from which really all life, all Creation proceeds." This is the Alpha and Omega of which Plotinus said: "You ask me: how can we know the Infinite? I answer, not by reason. It is the office of reason to distinguish and define. The Infinite therefore cannot be ranked among its objects. You can only apprehend the Infinite . . . by entering into *a state in which you are your finite self no longer.* This is . . . the liberation of your mind from finite consciousness. When you cease to be finite you become one with the Infinite. . . . You realize the union, the identity." Anyone who feels like it can verify the facts. The mystics always have.

It will be seen that their psychology is based on the incontrovertible fact of man's double nature, *Zwei Seelen,* that Faust knew so well. This is part of the traditional view everywhere, from which our own naturalistic psychologies are a deviation. The paradox of man, the pull of opposite tendencies and impulses, the crown of thorns of our divided being and the crown of redemption through suffering and sacrifice, the mechanical wheel of Nature (*Prakriti*) and the freedom of the Person (*Purusha,* the Witness Self) are known to every seeker, is in fact one of the bonds that bind the invisible brotherhood. It needs no ghost from the grave, or the clinics of Vienna, to tell us that, biologically and existentially, we belong almost wholly to a mechanic, animal and libidinal universe. But if that were all and this other, mystic or spiritual possibility were not, the life of contented animals would have done as well. But, as the wise have always insisted, there is such a possibility, or door of escape. A shift in the fields of perception that opens up a different, and more truly human prospect, "windows through which the mind looks out upon a more extensive and inclusive world," as James said. This is not a matter of faith alone, but of works, for the experience profoundly modifies both attitude and action.

Two methods for achieving this—the escape from the flame of separation, as Rumi puts it—suggest themselves: detachment and transference. The mystics are not asking for freedom in order to do what they please, they are not Egotistically Sublime. As the *Theologica Germanica* has it:

"So long as man seeketh his own highest good, *because* it is his, he will never find it." If our will is forever caught in the act there is no freedom for man as agent. He is forever bound. It is only in so far as a man may stand back, watch and control his impulses that he has some chance to know and be the free self within. In most traditional cultures we have, therefore, as a matter of rule, emphasis on discrimination, or contemplative withdrawal and non-attachment. In the classic formula of the *Upanishads:* "The good is one thing, the pleasant another; these two, having different objects, chain a man. It is well with him who clings to the good, he who chooses the pleasant misses his end." For all who wish to explore reality, the reality of self, the advice holds, in fact, imposes itself. This has been sometimes misunderstood and led to negative results, even among practitioners. In itself this is a stage, of self-vision. In the Indian system of *Samkhya* psychology, upon which the practice of yoga is so largely based, the concept of *Sakshi,* or Witness Self, plays a central role. We hear echoes of it in Henry David Thoreau. In *Solitude* he writes: "With thinking we may be beside ourselves in a sane sense. By a conscious effort of the mind we can stand aloof from actions and their consequences; and all things, good and bad, go by us like a torrent. We are not wholly involved in Nature. I may be either the drift-wood in the stream, or Indra in the sky looking down on it. I *may* be affected by a theatrical exhibition; on the other hand, I *may not* be affected by an actual event which appears to concern me much more. I only know myself as a human entity; the scene, so to speak, of thoughts and affections; and am sensible of a certain doubleness by which I can stand as remote from myself as from another. However intense my experience, I am conscious of the presence and criticism of a part of me, which, as it were, is not a part of me, but a spectator, sharing no experience, but taking note of it; and that is no more I than it is you. When the play, it may be the tragedy, of life is over, the spectator goes his way. It was a kind of fiction, a work of the imagination only, so far as he was concerned. This doubleness may easily make us poor neighbors and friends sometimes." In psychical research, Gardner Murphy reports, "out-of-the-body experiences (and)...phenomena appear to be real...and consistent with a modern conception of the unity of the living system in which mental phenomena, such as changed conceptions of the self, sense of identification with the universe, tendency to undergo bilocation (in which one looks down on one's own body and feels that the observer and the observed body are two different and equally real things), are experiences not very far from the known terrain of general psychology."[12]

Another related method, or another way things happen, is to transfer the center of personality from the ego to the Self, the Self that is one in all men, the uniting factor. As Evelyn Underhill has it, "a spiritual life is simply a life in which all that we do comes from the center, is anchored in God." It is easy to understand, why, as part of today's tragedy:

> Things fall apart; the centre cannot hold;
> Mere anarchy is loosed upon the world . . . .

The idea of such transference, or replacement, appears in most ethical systems, but is based on and sanctioned by mystical psychology, for otherwise it would not make much sense. Witnesses to its reality are to be found in all ages and periods. Not I but the Christ in me, wrote St. John. Whether we live or whether we die we are the Lord's, said St. Paul. Even for Arthur Koestler, "The I had ceased to exist." (It must have been marvelous, if it did.) How the lack of our understanding the need for such transference of the center of personality vitiates large areas of self-centered modern living will be seen from the following sober analysis of two clear-eyed psychologists:

> All feelings about one's value and worth, about what one can or cannot do are embodied in the Ego. So distorted are they, that the Ego is always a false image of the Self . . . a psychological shell encasing the Self. Every human being is unconsciously shut up within a system of mistaken ideas and feelings which thwart the fullest expression of the powers of the Self. The individual is limited, also, by the defects of the culture of his time.
>
> One basic task of man is the removal of this shell. A life-long problem. . . . But we must distinguish between an intellectual insight into the broad fact that the Ego is only our second, not our real nature—and the actual breakdown of the shell (is what we need) . . . . In the end, it seems that nothing short of the severest kind of pressure is enough to shatter the shell.
>
> This drastic experience we call the major crisis. . . . It should be welcomed . . . for through it we may move into the joy and peace that comes from releasing the Self within from the limitations of its shell into the creative, productive, courageous, loving expressions of which it is capable. This is indeed the abundant life.[13]

Jung's probings into the mysteries of the psyche have revealed that "the birth of the Self signifies for the conscious personality not only a displacement of the previous psychological center, but also as a consequence therefore a completely altered view and attitude towards life, a 'transvaluation' in the fullest sense of the word." Zen

Buddhism brings, or brought back, the same affirmation, in almost identical language: "The individual shell in which my personality is so solidly encased explodes at the moment of Satori. Not necessarily that I get united with a greater being than myself or absorbed in it, but my individuality which I found rigidly held together and definitely separate from other individual existence . . . melts away into something indescribable, something which is of a quite different order from what I am accustomed to."[14]

Much, if not all, of our misery is due to this inability and unwillingness to make the necessary psychological change and adjustment. Not to be born is the best, was the Greek version of tragedy. But not to be re-born is even worse. This transfer, or re-birth, is the inner sense of baptism, initiation and Brahmanic culture, the culture of the "twice-born", to which modern psychical research seems to be pointing again. "The discovery of a nonphysical element in personality, therefore, makes all the difference in the world to ethical values," writes J. B. Rhine. "Its proof of a nonphysical property in man allows a logical case to be made for volitional freedom. Without free will the idea of moral judgment would be meaningless. . . . Machines do not have free wills."[15] This is our only way of escaping the tiresome and frustrating round of a sensate culture about to end with a bang.

Mystical psychology is, however, not to be confused with stoicism and world-weariness, though there may be some common ground between the two. There is no question, writes Waite in *Lights of Western Mysticism*, that the end of Mysticism was reached by the method of ascetic life, during many past centuries. That is so, both in the east and in the west. The soul's energies thrive when the body's desires are feeblest, wrote one of the most distinguished of early Christians. But are the desires feeble or kept in check till they become feeble? And is sublimation not to be thought of? Mysticism, basically a technique of transference and transcendence, is not a tired or resolute indifference to the slings and arrows of fortune, including the dubious advantage of having a body clamoring for its own separate need. A higher formula of reconciliation, other than what the ascetics have to offer, must be possible, even if it is not easy. Whatever happens, the individual must change his stance, his outlook and gain a different, an inner view of things. In the end, and even long before the end is reached, he remains not only unmoved by what happens on the surface, in the world and in himself, but he might also gain the power to transmute all experience into its opposite. This is not easy to do, but some power or promise of it can come early, enough to create that faith which helps one to continue. From all this it follows that for his happiness the mystic does not depend upon objects, material possessions, or social approval, all of which may be taken away. He interiorizes and etherealizes his values, tries perhaps what is the only worthwhile and successful transvaluation of values, of which some frenzied and imbalanced thinkers, like Nietzsche, have caught a hurried glimpse without being able to actualize it in their own lives. The presence of the mystical individual is a proof of the inspiring actuality of such a transfer or remaking of man. It is in the best sense a criticism of life, the kind that most of us lead. It is the best criticism of the actual in terms of the ideal. Seek ye, as we have sought, and you will see what we have seen, such is the mystic promise and challenge, and, as Dean Inge is there to tell us, "it is not wise to disregard it."

The individual, then, is not ego but the self. In the daily business of living this, of course, is not the view we take of ourselves. For the most part our identification with the ego is complete. We treat ourselves as separate beings that somehow exist in a world external to ourselves and, if we are rigorously inclined, both are made to depend on an extra-cosmic God, an outsider. Naturally, in order to know or "realize" the extra-cosmic deity one has to abandon both world and individual and so one finds

> Its liberation and immobile calm
> A void recall of being from Time-made things,
> Not the self-vision of Reality.

So at least most ascetic disciplines have viewed man's becoming in the world, in terms of an ultimate rejection. To quote Sri Aurobindo again:

> In the beginning an unknowing Force,
> In the middle an embodied striving soul,
> In the end a silent spirit denying life.

But such a trenchant division or tearing away is not the only, as it is certainly not an ideal, view of things. It is quite possible to look upon the Transcendent itself as one with the universe, as something that does not exclude either the world or the individual. Of course the illumination of the individual continues to be necessary but it does not lead to an exit or excision from the universal movement. Individual realization or salvation can have little sense if the world itself has no value, no *raison d'être*. In other words, we must accept "the many-sidedness of the manifestation even while we assert the unity of the Manifested." As Lancelot Whyte has pointed out, today there seems to be a marked tendency, among thinkers, "to investigate experimentally whether the Oriental conception of multiple unity is not a more demonstrable apprehension of reality than the aspects under which Western thought has hitherto envisaged it." Maybe "Neither the Eastern emphasis on an undifferentiated unity of process nor the Western stress on specific differences can carry the human tradition through this century. The time has come for a new elegance: a unity of process seen in all particular forms and reconciling their differences. A fresh stress must be laid on universal principles in order to restore a proper equilibrium. But once again there is no balance in the dialectic. East and West are not on an equal footing. The West has made the modern world and the West must redeem it. Until Western science recognizes the formative process no fundamental advance is possible."[16] It is this fundamental advance, in terms of a formative process, which the greater mystics represent. They are the true avant-garde. In the spiritual experience the conscious individual, the ego, becomes the superficial point at which the awareness of unity emerges; it is possible to extend this awareness to include all others, which would be the most real liberation—from all limits. The individual would still and always remain, but his range and content, quality and effectiveness would be totally changed.

In the inspired words of an Eastern sage: "The liberation of the individual soul is the keynote of the definitive divine action; it is the primary divine necessity and the pivot on which all else turns. It is the point of Light at which the intended complete self-manifestation in the Many begins to emerge. But the liberated soul extends its perception of unity horizontally as well as vertically. Its unity with the transcendent One is incomplete without its unity with the cosmic Many. And that lateral unity translates itself by multiplication, a reproduction of its own liberated state at other points of the Multiplicity. The divine soul reproduces itself in similar liberated souls as the animal reproduces itself in similar bodies. Therefore whenever even a single soul is liberated, there is a tendency to an extension and even to an outburst of the same divine self-consciousness in other individual souls of our terrestrial humanity and—who knows—perhaps even beyond the terrestrial consciousness. Where shall we fix the limit of that extension? Is it altogether a legend which says of the Buddha that as he stood on the threshold of Nirvana, of the Non-Being, his soul turned back and took the vow never to make the irrevocable crossing so long as there was a single being upon earth undelivered from the knot of suffering, from the bondage of the ego?"[17]

To us, standing on the "flat land" of the ego all this reads like a suprarational mystery and so it is indeed. But it is obviously a part of human experience, known and felt, again and again, by the masters of the inner life, the human evolution. It is also not impossible to imagine and has formed part of a persistent dream and an ideal. Our empirical consciousness, the little I, is a construction, a limitation and a practical selection from world-being. But the real individual, the great I, exists too, though it exceeds the limits of the little ego. The differentiation still holds, but it no longer separates. It is the sweetness of the Same that holds all. The individual is still necessary, but this individual unites or integralizes three states of the being—individual, universal and transcendental. He is the true Person: He am I, *So'ham*.[18] If in the end "the individual has the power of self-discovery and entrance into the transcendent eternity and his liberation has so great an importance, it must be because he too is a reality of the Transcendence; but has to discover himself individually, because his individuality has also some truth of itself in the Transcendence which is veiled from it and which it has to recover." To recover the reality of this hidden Transcendent ("the guest within," to use the Vedic phrase), the Self as Freedom is, then, the nature and destiny of the individual, what he is here for.

There would appear to be nothing contradictory in such a unitarian, comprehensive view of an Essence carrying a multitude of existences, a status of the Infinite supporting an endless series of the finite, the Individual seen as a self-expression of the Universal and the Transcendent at once. To a logic that is not bound to the dogmas of our proud and self-denying reason, there is nothing unusual in this unity or relation of the individual with the two other terms of existence, the universal and the transcendent. It is the simplest of mysteries, the simplest and perhaps the ultimate.

Nothing increases more the value of the individual in the world than this view of existence and destiny. The individual remains, but with an enhanced significance. In the words of the youthful champion of the "outsider" cult: "The solution, as always, is for the individual Outsider to continue to bring a new consciousness to birth. . . . The burden remains upon the individual Outsider."[19] The only difference being that the mystic Outsider is also an Insider, in so far as he has found his relation with the Real. He is not a maladjusted exhibitionist, whose picture of freedom is suspiciously close to being a praise of folly. The importance of the individual is dual, so to speak. In Sri Aurobindo's words:

"It is through him that the cosmic spirit organises the collective units and makes them self-expressive and progressive and through him that it raises Nature from the Inconscience to the Superconscience and exalts it to meet the Transcendent. The progress of the mind, the growth of the soul, even of the mind and soul of the collectivity, depends on the individual, or his sufficient freedom and independence. In the crowd the individual loses his sense of direction and becomes a cell of the mass body. . . . He has to stand apart,[21] affirm his separate reality in the whole, his own mind emerging from the common mentality, even as his body has developed something unique and recognisable in the common physicality. He has even, in the end, to retire into himself to find himself, and it is only when he has found himself that he can be one with all."

"It is because of the spiritual Person, the Divinity in the individual, that the perfection or the liberation—salvation, as it is called in the West—has to be individual and not collective; for whatever perfection of the collectivity is to be sought after, can come only by the perfection of the individuals who constitute it. It is because the individual is That, that to find himself is his greatest necessity. In his complete surrender and self-giving to the Supreme it is he who finds perfect self-finding in a perfect self-offering. In the abolition of the mental, vital, physical ego, even of the spiritual ego, it is the formless and limitless Individual that has the peace and joy of its escape into its own infinity. In the experience that he is nothing and no one, or everything and everyone, or the One which is beyond all things and absolute, it is the individual . . . that effectuates himself. To get beyond the ego is imperative, but one cannot get beyond the Self—except by finding it supremely, universally. For the Self is not the ego, it is one with the All and the One and in finding it, it is the All and the One that we discover in our self: the contradiction, the separation disappears, but the self, the spiritual reality remains, united with the One and the All by that delivering disappearance.[20]

"All man's age-long effort, his action, society, art, ethics, science, religion, all the manifold activities by which he expresses and increases his mental, vital, physical, spiritual existence, are episodes in the vast drama of this endeavour of Nature and have behind their limited apparent aims no other true sense or foundation. For the individual to arrive at the divine universality and supreme identity, live in it, possess it, to be, know, feel and express that alone in all his being, consciousness, energy, delight of being is what the ancient seers of the Veda meant by knowledge; that was the Immortality which they set before man as his culmination."

An obscure feeling impels the modern world in the same direction. If only it could be a more conscious and concerted effort!

For how different is all this from our own knowing sets delving deep into the abysses of the Existential and Irrational Man! Not to speak of the good mixer, the well-adjusted man (see "Be not conformed to this world," says the mystic, "but be ye transformed by the renewing of your mind"), the happy consumer, the go-getter, all that makes our world what it is, the shirt of Nessus which we cannot strip off, as Jung said. He had also a feeling, not without reason, that "science has destroyed even the refuge of the inner life. What was once a sheltering heaven has become a place of terror,"—the analyst's couch. But the need of the inner life remains, though that is not all that there is to it. "The inner life has a supreme importance and the outer has a value only in so far as it is expressive of the inner status," says a master whom we have quoted before. "However the man of spiritual realisation lives and acts and behaves, in all ways of his being and acting . . . he lives in the Divine. In our present life of Nature, in our externalised surface existence, it is the world that seems to create us; but in the turn to the spiritual life it is we who must create ourselves and our world. In this new formula of creation, the inner life becomes of the first importance and the rest can be only its expression and outcome. It is this, indeed, that is indicated by our own strivings towards perfection, the perfection of our own soul and mind and life and the perfection of the life of the race. For we are given a world which is obscure, ignorant, material, imperfect and our external conscious being is itself created by its energies, the pressure, the moulding operations of the vast mute obscurity, by physical birth, by environment, by a training through the impacts and shocks of life; and yet we are vaguely aware of something that is there in us or seeking to be, something other than what has been thus made, a spirit self-existent, self-determining, pushing the nature towards the image of its own occult perfection or Idea of perfection. There is something that grows in answer to this demand, that strives to become the image of a divine Somewhat, and is impelled also to labour at the world outside that has been given to it and remake that too in a greater image, in the image of its own spiritual and mental and vital growth, to make our world into something created according to our own mind and self-conceiving spirit, something new, harmonious, perfect."[22]

The idea of perfection is moved in two different directions: towards self-improvement and the improvement of the environment, change from within and change from without. It is easy to see that a balance and not conflict of these two impulses is what we need, though it is obvious that the inner change must lead. "The inner life once created, to convert our whole surface being, our thought, feeling, action in the world, into a perfect power of that inner life, must be our other preoccupation. . . . A perfected human world cannot be created by men or composed of men who are themselves imperfect.

"To become ourselves is the one thing to be done; but the true ourselves is that which is within us, and to exceed our outer self of body, life and mind is the condition for this highest being, which is our true and divine being, to become self-revealed and active. It is only by growing within and living within that we can find it; once that is done, to create from there the spiritual or divine mind, life and body and through this instrumentalisation to arrive at the creation of a world which shall be the true environment of a divine living,—this is the final object that Force of Nature has set before us. This then is the first necessity, that the individual, each individual, shall discover the spirit, the divine reality, within him and express that in all his being and living. A divine life must be first and foremost an inner life, for since the outward must be the expression of what is within, there can be no divinity in the outer existence if there is not the divinization of the inner being. The Divinity in man dwells veiled in his spiritual center, there can be no such thing as self-exceeding for man or a higher issue for his existence if there is not in him the reality of an external self and spirit."[23]

These things, the discovery of the self and the re-creation of an outer world, "the true environment of a divine living", are impossible without an inner living. It is in answer to this imperative need or condition that the spiritual or spiritually-minded individual has had to withdraw into himself, sometimes moving out of society altogether. The crowd or a crowded social life is not the best locale to cultivate this kind of inwardness. To that extent a mass culture is self-condemned. As Hocking writes, "Solitude, I say, is the essence of mysticism: and I add, the basis of its supreme social importance . . . (for) Mysticism in its true character is precisely the redemption of solitude."[24] It is necessary to add that no individual is exhausted by social adjustment, there is in him something more than social. He belongs not merely to society nor even to humanity, but to something over and above all these, to Infinity. The romantics were not so wrong in calling him a pilgrim of eternity. When, as has happened frequently, society forgets or forbids this, the individual, in an effort to assert his identity, has either to retire or rebel, or both, and then we have an unfortunate and unfinished civil war between the spiritual seeking and society. Luckily, "mysticism can provide its own corrective."[25] though it is hardly to be denied "that the mystics (sometimes) find themselves in bad company."[26] But, as we have throughout maintained, the individual is always necessary, he has a duty to perform which no one else can do for him. It is he who hears the call and must answer it.

His *ultimate* allegiance can never be to a state or a nation but the Truth above and within, which while it includes these middle terms of his existence soars beyond these into a realm of value all its own and which no society has, as yet, succeeded in embodying. It is, as yet, a promise and a possibility—the hope of a transformed, divine life for all people.

An occasional eccentricity or glorified selfishness does not represent the individual response at its best. Even "the opposition between mysticism and institutional life...is real but not final; mysticism is beyond institutions but not necessarily hostile to them. . . . What the mystic rejects is not the claim that the established forms of social life are necessary for a complete life but the claim that they are sufficient."[27] In any case, the individual as he moves towards his spiritual nature and freedom realizes also his identity and freedom with others. This shows itself, as in the ideal of the Bodhisattva, in an increase in goodwill and charity. The spiritually-realized being, the liberated individual is preoccupied, says the *Gita*, with the good of all being. His ethics is grounded in beyond ethics. What the mystics learn in contemplation they give out in love. The "organised lovelessness" of our own days can be counteracted only by the strivings of the mystics and saints and not by efforts of a Welfare State or the not-so-hidden persuaders of Madison Avenue. Only when one is free can one free others. The individual in freeing himself frees others. But, as St. Bernard said, no one can comprehend what it is, save he who has experienced it. As Max Scheler used to say, "The history of the men who have been models of humanity form the centre of the soul of history, and it is by the ideal that they represent that we judge existing humans. . . . This is why each one of us looks into the heart of the saint for his own salvation." In the penetrating words of Simone Weil: "We live in an age which is quite without precedent: today there is nothing in being a saint. We need a saintliness proper to the present moment, a new saintliness which is also without a precedent. The world needs saints of genius, just as a city stricken by plague needs doctors. Where there is a need there is an obligation."

It is the distinction of the individual to recognize that obligation above all others. It is the only heroism that matters, perhaps the only one left to us, the right 'to be'.

But individual salvation without the social is incomplete. The collective, community of communities, has a truth and power of its own. The soul is a society. As Sri Aurobindo put it: If there is hope for man, why should there not be hope for mankind?

VI

The Ideal Group

Shalt thou be saved and hear the whole world cry?

BIRDS of the same feather flock together. Even Jesus had spoken of his "little flock". But in the development of mysticism the lonely birds have been even more common and preceded the flocks. There have been "Outsiders" long before the term became popular. "The Outsider only exists," says the modern champion of the term and the creed, "because our civilization has lost its realization." To believe Mr. Wilson—which is not necessary—the outsider is the salt of the earth and has always been, the hero of our time, the spiritual heir of the prophets.[1] It is his other diagnosis, of the Outsider's role in the contemporary scene, that seems to be more acceptable: "a symptom of our time and age...the Outsider is the key to the decline of the West." But, of course, Wilsonian Outsiders are not always mystics or even mystical. The true mystic is as much "in" as "out". In fact he is "in" when he is "out" and *vice versa*.

Most mature communities have recognized the role of such individuals and profited by their presence and example. Nor have these men themselves always or often dwelt apart, though this seems to be a widely-held view. As Evelyn Underhill wrote: "By the very term 'mystic' we indicate a certain aloofness from the crowd, suggest that he is in possession of a secret which the community as a whole does not and cannot share; that he lives at levels to which they cannot rise. I think that much of the distrust with which he is often regarded comes from this sense of his independence of the herd." And the herd knows how to hit back. So, it would seem, does the lonely pioneer. His vision of God leaves him little choice. For, if "the work of the Church ends when the knowledge of God begins," mysticism cannot but be un-institutional or anti-institutional. It is, as Dean Inge has noted, personal religion in its inmost essence. The mystic, says another philosophic student of the subject, "has discovered a source of new values. . . .(He) confronts the existing order not with the intent of pure destruction but with a new standard of what human nature really needs. In effect the mystic says to society: Here I stand with my own vision of truth, my own ideal of human destiny, my own power of judgment. How many institutions can stand the test?[2]

Such being the fact, Underhill's defense of institutional mysticism, or the Church, fails to carry conviction. She feels and would like us to believe that "the great mystics are loyal children of the great religious institutions," that for the mystic "it is better. . .that he should be within a church than outside it." Without being offensive, it seems that she knows what is better for the mystics than the mystics themselves knew. She goes on to say that the mystic achievement "makes more valid and more actual to us the assumptions upon which external religion is built." This is surely half the story and a poor defense. For if mystical experience justifies "external religion," which may be doubted, it at the same time shows up its limitations no less. If, as she claims, "the great mystics were faithful sons of the great religions", then why were the Sufis persecuted? Even Ramakrishna was a thorn in the side of the hidebound conservatives and remained unacceptable to the orthodox till such time as it became impossible to keep him out, and a new order grew up round him. So, when Underhill suggests that "the view which regards the mystic as a spiritual anarchist receives little support from history" we can only beg to differ. For what she calls "the support and discipline of organized religion" is often the very thing which not a few of the mystics, including "mystics of the church", have been kicking against, gently or violently, but almost invariably. One reason for this is that the mystics know, far better than the conformist crowd, the difference between "Historical Christians" and "new men". In the end even Underhill has to admit the presence of two types of mystics in the Christian fold, the rebel and the law-abiding, the heretical and the orthodox. Both types must be recognized without any attempt at moral judgment. Mystics *within* the fold are also a fact, though we shall probably never know the whole history of that uneasy adjustment, between vision and authority.

But when the mystics deliberately and sometimes defiantly kept away from the group, or formed special groups of their own, such "distancing" has to be looked into carefully, not necessarily from the point of view of those whom they tried to avoid and who are therefore more likely to misunderstand than those who have a sympathy for all ways of the spirit, including what might appear wayward ways. In this one must distinguish between "beyond-man" and "hostile-to-man". No doubt the variety of mystical experience and experiment contains both types. But why have mystics been, or thought to have been, such "oddballs", owing so little to social sense and responsibility? Why then should society tolerate their anti-social antics? Or is there more to it than we have suspected? And how are the mystics related to religious groups? And why were these not enough? And what about the mystical groups? How are they to be related to other forms of organization?

Most people would perhaps agree with "the commonest of criticisms" brought against the mystics, that they "represent an unsocial type of religion, that their spiritual enthusiasms are personal and individual, and that they do not share or value the corporate life and institutions of the church or community to which they belong." In fact it has not always been a case of simple and invariable opposition: mystic versus society, or "My kingdom is not of this world." An appearance of conflict, even an occasional need for it, must be admitted. But this should not be allowed to disturb our sense of proportion. We must find out why this is or should have been so, and hope for happier adjustments.

It is well-known that each human tendency moves towards its own extreme or absolute. So does the spirit of mystic withdrawal, cutting across all social duties and mores. At the other end of the spectrum we have the image of the Welfare State or the Big Brother. In the end such extremes meet and correct themselves. So, let us hope, it might be with the mystics and society, both going their own ways would meet in the end. For they need each other, even if, like those who need each other, they sometimes get on each other's nerves. The monk, the recluse, the Timonlike misanthrope, the "rhinoceros", wandering *bhiksu* or the lonely hermit ploughing his lonely furrow, seeking his solitary salvation, is a familiar type, more familiar than the other type, which has existed too. The voice of wisdom and admonition has not ceased: Shalt thou be saved and hear the whole world cry? Even Lenin used to say that the cry of a single child in distress condemned the whole world. The idea has been expressed, more than once, by William Blake:

A robin redbreast in a cage
Puts all Heaven in a rage . . . .
A skylark wounded in the wing,
A cherubim does cease to sing . . . .
The beggar's dog and the widow's cat
Feed them, and thou wilt grow fat . . . .
Every tear from every eye
Becomes a babe in eternity.

It would be an inexplicable paradox if the mystics, who are at least spiritually sensitive, should be unconcerned about their fellow human beings. So, why did they leave family, society, everything? What was the strange compulsion that forced them to this course of action? We shall probably never know. For these things cannot be studied as one studies "cases". One must go the whole way, at least part of it, before one can report about the lay of the land and where it leads to, and if it does not reach back to the point of departure, by another route as it were.

The so-called flight, escape, renunciation of the individual mystic is but an arc, the circle is wider and inclusive. Withdrawal without Return makes no sense. Really, "we come back to the same world, the old-time tasks, changed, yet everything is different."[3] Or, as Boehme said, in the mystic experience the world will not be destroyed, but re-made. The lives of the great saints and mystics, among whom are to be counted nearly all the founders of what are called the higher religions of mankind, show the working of this principle clearly enough. In his *Study of History* Toynbee has rightly drawn attention to this fact: "Creative personalities when they are taking the mystic path which is their highest spiritual level . . . belong to the duality of movement we call . . .

91

withdrawal and return. The withdrawal makes possible forthe personality to realize powers within itself which might have remained dormant if he had not been released for the time being from his social toils and turmoils. . .but a transfiguration in solitude can have no purpose, and perhaps even no meaning, except as a prelude to the return of the transfigured personality into the social milieu out of which he originally came. . . .The return is the essence of the whole movement as well as its final cause." In the more poetic language of Edward Carpenter: "Then to return to be used—and then only to be rightly used, to be free and open for ever." And so those who can look beyond the apparent conflict between mystics and society know that the lives of these pioneers into the Unknown are not entirely unrelated with our social existence and destiny. Perhaps in these lives "more easily than elsewhere, we may discern the principles which do or should govern the relation of the individual to the community." Even the supra-social helps the social, if we will but allow, that is understand.

In truth mystics do not reject society. What they are trying to do is to start a new research, for a new formula, of ascent and integration, and because it is something new it will not be easy to fit this into the old pattern which is often not plastic enough for the purpose. They have seen the vision of a new order and cannot, would not, deny its clear imperatives. In every age and in nearly every society we come across men and women, sometimes even groups of people, on whom the hold of convention has visibly weakened, who have lost faith in existing social ideals and practice and who, sooner or later, step out. Examples of such individual withdrawal or escape, protest or non-conformity have come down from the earliest ages, from Egypt, Persia, India, China, even from the primitive tribes. These were the born ascetics, the monastics, holy men, often credited with supernormal

92

power and insight, who were among the most highly respected members of the tribe, even though apparently they did not "belong". It will be a mistake to look upon them merely as curiosities of cultural anthropology, as many of our "rational", "scientific" investigators were apt to do. If these men gave nothing back to society, as some would like to think, what about the leaders of modern society? Are we so sure how posterity, if there is one, will look back upon our captains of industry, the bosses of big business, and, above all, our experts of aerial and bacterial warfare, these natural leaders of to-day, men of light and learning? The earlier ascetics had a philosophy, a point of view and a code of conduct which has lost none of its edge. We can better them, if we dare, but we cannot bypass them, except to our own discredit. Really, we little know either their goal or their methods, what aims they pursued or what "orchestral evolution's theme" they serve. Misunderstanding is a small price for the pearl of great price that they seek, not, be it said, for themselves alone, but for all men, even those that deny and oppose. In the sober language of Lecomte du Noüy: "The purely human conflict (of evolution) is born from this permanent bitter struggle which has lost none of its violence today."[4] The conflict continues, still "worthy to raise issues." That, incidentally, is one of its great services to a somnolent society, dead to ideals, and on its way to a Dead End.

Not many have responded to the call of the mystics. They were and remain a minority, but a creative minority. Here is one of them speaking: "The mass of humanity evolves slowly, containing in itself all stages of the evolution from the material and vital man to mental man. A small minority has pushed beyond the barriers, opening the doors to occult and spiritual knowledge and preparing the ascent of the evolution beyond mental man into spiritual and supramental being. Sometimes this minority has exercised an enormous influence as in Vedic India, Egypt, or, according to tradition, in Atlantis, and determined the civilization of the race, giving it a strong stamp of the spiritual or the occult; sometimes they stood apart in their separate schools or orders, not directly influencing a civilization which was sunk in material ignorance or in chaos and darkness or in the hard external enlightenment which rejects spiritual knowledge."[5] This ought to give us pause. We who pretend to judge may be among the accused. A little thinking will show that echoes of that earlier mystical thought can still be heard, for such as have ears to hear. It is only the forms of thought or practice that have changed, as they ought to, but not the spirit.

Of course no thought is needed to see that in an age of consumer economy and conspicuous waste the ideal of the ascetic will sound archaic and quite unacceptable. And yet—who does not know?—a certain kind of asceticism or high discipline is indispensable for any superior activity or achievement. Making money, waging war, and going to the moon are no exception, however questionable might be the motives for such noble undertakings by the well-adjusted majority. Modern science itself would have been impossible without subtle and special discipline of body and mind, a faith in the unseen. The ascetic we have always with us. It is not enough to point to the excesses and absurdities of the tribe. *Mutatis mutandis*, one might point to the destructive intent and application of science, and condemn the whole show as a diabolic and insufferable perversion of the will that is no better, indeed much worse, than the absurdities of a few ascetics. Two can play at that game.

Today, when we are living no longer "in the delicious intoxication induced by the early successes of science, but in a rather grisly morning after," the life of the spirit should call for far more careful and intelligent consideration than what we have given it so far. Society being what it has always been, the isolation of the mystic, who is often but not necessarily an ascetic, has been a condition of his experiment with truth. The fact that so many, among them some of the best that society has ever produced—the fact is conceded even by such open and confirmed critics of the mystical and monastic life as Gibbon and Frazer—had to move out of the society of their own periods is a sufficient criticism of the un-spiritual social organizations under which they had to live, and rightly refused to live. The fact did not escape Underhill. In the very first paragraph of her well-known and sympathetic study of Mysticism she could not help noting that very frequently the mystics have been driven to their position in spite of, not because of, society; and she points out how "branches of the human family produce sporadically and often in the teeth of adverse circumstances a curious and definite type of personality." As Tillich has noted, the religious answer has always the character of "in spite of." As regards Christian mysticism, this is what Gerald Heard has to say: "The mystical tradition of Christianity ... has never been appreciated save by the few, never systematized into techniques, and always suspected by the authorities—the theologians and administrators—and by the masses. And not only has it been intuitive and esoteric, but almost an underground movement, always subject to the accusation of antinomianism and heresy."[6] The antinomy was inevitable and yet we have permitted ourselves the optimism that a time may come when mysticism will be normal and part of the social setting. Not, let us hope, through the use of drugs[7] but a better understanding and the availability of disciplines within the social framework. It is true there is sometimes a certain defiance in the ascetic's code and gesture, a kind of noli me tangere. If he cannot win, he will not submit either. If he cannot integrate, he will at least affirm.

Whether the Kingdom of God is here or hereafter, it has

first to be reached within and then adjusted to the outer world. Without going within there is no hope or chance of that discovery. Faced with a crisis—and such crises have been fairly frequent, indeed to the mystic and the saint life is a perpetual crisis[8]—the responsible individual has two ways open to him: he can use violence or he can use ways of peace. He can be either a Lenin or a Gandhi. That will depend on what kind of man he is and the thoughts he has. Both the ways are forms of radical, revolutionary import, and both have been tried, again and again. It is sheer blindness to say that only military and political revolutions deserve to be considered and that the ways of the mystics and saints count for nothing. Perhaps "More violence, less revolution." Who knows? Great changes in human life and attitude do not take place with the beat of drums, or dropping of bombs. "Smash or go on to higher things. So far no civilization has ever met the challenge successfully."[9] It is easier to smash and if no civilization has met the challenge successfully, a small minority has, on behalf of a society that has almost disowned them and paid them with nothing but misuse and misunderstanding. An Age of Noise and Nuisance can hardly be expected to appreciate the more human and humane ways of the mystics. A grasping civilization can hardly believe that there have been men who have preferred to be left out or stay behind, men who have spurned the advances of the bitch goddess (the only one left in the pantheon), who welcome sacrifice and still do. Our values must change before we can talk intelligently about mysticism and the nature of the help offered by it to our society. St. Joan spoke a little too much like a Shavian heroine when she told the people that they did not deserve a saint. But there was some truth behind that show of temper.

What, one wonders, are the chances of a mystic group, or a group of devoted individuals as Huxley once described it? What are the chances of a monastic order in the world today? Not so little as those who have never thought about these matters might imagine. Some remarks, chosen without much care, will show this. "If the work is to be done and it is clear that unless it is done, the state of the world is likely to become progressively worse—it must be done by associations of devoted individuals," was Huxley's view in *Ends and Means*. "At any given moment of history it is the function of associations of devoted individuals to undertake tasks which clearsighted people perceive to be necessary, but which nobody else is willing to perform." That "dark sun", D. H. Lawrence, had once written: "I want you to form the nucleus of a community which shall start a new life among us. . . .Let us be good all together, instead of just in the privacy of our chambers. . . .The question now is how we shall fulfill our declaration 'God is'. For all our life is based on the assumption that God is not." The history of aesthetic utopias is of course much longer. For instance the ideal community on the banks of the Susquehana (chosen for its beautiful name) to which Coleridge and his friends in the end did not go. Or this from the early Yeats: "I planned a mystical order that should buy or hire the castle, and keep it as a place where its members could retire for a while for contemplation, and where we might establish mysteries like those of Eleusis or Samothrace. . . .I had an unshakable conviction that invisible gates would open, as they opened for Blake, as they opened for Swedenborg, as they opened for Boehme, and that this philosophy would find its manuals of devotion in all imaginative literature." Though these artistic dreams have a way of remaining unfulfilled promises they show the persistence of an attitude which it would be idle to deny.

Here is a version from a more serious source. "If we had to wait for the mass of humanity to reach a state of harmony, unity and aspiration, strong enough to bring down the Light and change the material conditions and the movement of Nature, there would be little hope. But there is a possibility that an individual or a small group or limited number may achieve the descent. It is not quantity or extension that matters."[10] Or, as Huxley has stated clearly enough: "At almost every period and in almost every country private individuals have associated for the purpose of initiating desirable changes and of working out for themselves a way of life superior to that of their contemporaries. In the preservation and development of civilization these groups of devoted individuals have played a very important part and are destined, I believe, to play a part no less important in the future."[11] Alexis Carrel, who had thought deeply over the whole problem, had this to say: "Revolutions often start with small groups in which the new tendencies ferment and grow. . . .In the past the efforts of isolated individuals caused the ascent of religion, science and education." And "Why should not some individuals sacrifice their lives to acquire the science indispensable to the making of man and of his environment? In fact, the task is extremely difficult. But minds capable of undertaking it can be discovered. . . . Men grow when inspired by a high purpose, when contemplating vast horizons. The sacrifice of oneself is not very difficult for one burning with the passion for a great adventure. And there is no more beautiful and dangerous adventure than the renovation of modern man." A new encounter with monasticism, or modified monasticism, is not unlikely. Perhaps that is what the age needs, above all.

The fact that the work of renovation is likely to be confined to small groups is not surprising. For "a group, although small, is capable of imposing upon its members rules of conduct modelled on military and monastic orders. Such a method is far from being new. Humanity

has already lived through periods when communities of
men or women separated from others and adopted strict
regulations, in order to attain their ideals. . . .Are we not
capable of repeating, in a different form, the accomplish-
ments of the monks, the knights, and the artisans of the
Middle Ages? Two essential conditions for the progress of
the individual are relative isolation and discipline. . . .It is
a well-established fact that discipline gives great strength
to man. An ascetic and mystic minority would rapidly acquire an irresistible power over the dissolute and degraded majority." Carrel, however, goes off at a tangent
when he adds, a little triumphantly, "Such a minority
would be in a position to impose, by persuasion or
perhaps by force, other ways of life upon the majority."
Now, that way error lies. The mystic does not "impose"
and never by force. It is a dangerous but attractive error.
The mystic is not a dictator in sheep's clothing, he is not a
persuader, subtle or crude, demanding the sacrifice of
your intelligence and individuality. He helps you to grow
into the ways of the Spirit, he does not first bind you in
order to make you free later. As Rufus Jones has pointed
out, "But it is an eternal law that there can be no *compulsion* in the realm of the spirit. It is essentially a world of
free creative choices."[12] Or as the psychologist, Allport,
puts it, "Though he is socially interdependent with others
in a thousand ways, yet no one else is able to provide him
with the faith he evolves nor prescribe for him his pact
with the cosmos."[13] After all, however useful a community of the faithful, of devoted individuals, each man must
work out his salvation alone. No man can free another. He
can only help.

But that such groups or orders are a possibility must be
granted. After a careful and sympathetic study of some of
the great founders of the Christian orders this is the conclusion of a scholar: "Indeed, a renewal of the Orders, in
their original intent, would be one of the most effective

aids in the spiritual conflicts of our times. . . .Another major possibility is the deliberate endeavour to create new
orders. . . .Difficult not to believe that it will be new
religious foundations that will transform our times. . . .
Unless the spirit of monasticism is injected into our society anew. . . .Deliverance from the distress of our times
can come only from small groups with the courage to remain small. . . .In the new religious foundations the
waters of mysticism are again beginning to flow." But, it
is as well to know that, "however much one may long for
new orders they cannot be artificially created. . . .What
is holy can never be commanded."[14] We do not create
fellowship deliberately, it has been said, rightly. Or, as
Dean Inge put it, institutionalism and mysticism have
always been uneasy bedfellows. The Buddha warned his
disciples against all "external refuge." In admitting, even
welcoming the possibility of new forms of monasticism we
must however be aware of the dangers of all such institutionalism, as the history of religious societies or institutions is there to show.

Today too many speak, cheerfully, of a return to
religion, what Sorokin has described as salvation in a
mild religious therapy. But this is not what the age needs
or is looking for. Referring to the so-called revival of
religion in American society and specifically to such in-
fluential apostles like Billy Graham and Norman Vincent
Peale, Tillich has shown how neither is an answer to the
religious question of the period. In a slightly different context Jung had observed: "The passionate interest in these
(psychic) movements arises undoubtedly from psychic
energy which can no longer be invested in obsolete forms
of religion. . . .The modern man abhors dogmatic postu-
lates taken on faith. . . .He holds them valid only in so far
as their knowledge-content seems in accord with his own
experience."[15] As the mystic sees it, there is—in Sri
Aurobindo's phrase—"a way to be opened that is still

blocked, not a religion to be founded." Or, as Hoffding has said, from being a pillar of fire in the van, "organized religion has become an ambulance trailing behind, picking up the weary and the worn." More explicitly: "If we look at the old religions in their social as apart from their individual aspect, we see that the use society made of them was only of their less spiritual parts. It made use of them to give an august, awful and would-be eternal sanction to a mass of customs and institutions, it made of them a veil of mystery against human questioning and a shield of darkness against the innovator. So far as it saw in religion a means of human salvation and perfection, it laid hands upon it at once to mechanize it, to catch the human soul and bind it on the wheels of a socio-religious machinery, to impose on it in the place of spiritual freedom an imperious yoke and an iron prison. It saddled upon the religious life of man a Church, a priesthood and a mass of ceremonies and set over it a pack of watchdogs under the name of creeds and dogmas, dogmas which one had to accept and obey under pain of condemnation to eternal hell by an eternal judge beyond, just as one had to accept and to obey the laws of society on pain of condemnation to temporal imprisonment or death by a mortal judge below. This false socialization of religion has been always the chief cause of its failure to regenerate mankind."* As Simone Weil put it, "Christ rejected the Devil's offer of the kingdom of this world. But the Church, His Bride, has succumbed to it." Dean Inge has noted that Church history is not pleasant reading. Institutional Churches are really secular corporations, molded to attract average humanity. Powerful Churches have gained the

*Sri Aurobindo, *The Human Cycle, the Idea of Human Unity & Self-Determination*, 4th ed. (N.Y.: International Publications Service, 1971).

upper hand by methods utterly opposed to the Spirit of Christ. As Berdyaeff says, men have set themselves to hate in the cause of love, to use compulsion in the name of freedom, and to become practicing materialists for the inculcation of spiritual principles.[16] The falsehood of the old social use of religion is shown by its effects, as Sri Aurobindo has pointed out. "History has exhibited more than once the coincidence of the greatest religious fervour and piety with the darkest ignorance, with an obscure squalor and long vegetation of the mass of human life, with the unquestioned reign of cruelty, injustice and oppression, or with the organization of the most ordinary, unaspiring and unraised existence hardly relieved by some touches of intellectual or half spiritual light on the surface, the end of all this a widespread revolt against the established religion as the keystone of the regnant falsehood, evil and ignorance. It is another sign when the too scrupulously exact observation of a socio-religious system and its rites and forms, which by the very fact of this misplaced importance begin to lose their sense and true religious value, becomes the law and the most prominent aim of religion rather than any spiritual growth of the individual and the race. And a great sign of the failure is when the individual is obliged to flee from society in order to find room for his spiritual growth; when finding human life given over to the unregenerate mind, life and body and the place of spiritual freedom occupied by the bonds of form, by Church and Shastra, by some law of the Ignorance, he is obliged to break away from all these to seek for growth into the spirit in the monastery, on the mountain-top, in the cavern, in the desert and the forest. When there is that division between life and the spirit, sentence of condemnation is passed upon human life."[17]

The freedom of the individual and the freedom of individual *sadhana* call for the most delicate handling and few societies have a good record to show. But while the individual as law unto himself has a tendency to run into unregulated fantasies and other excesses difficult to control or approve, the safety belt of prohibitive regulations is no answer either. If in deference to the safety of the type, or the group, society insists on conformity, something withers. And, either as symptom or protest, fanatics, fantasts and other signs appear on the horizon. Some leave society and elect silence. But, as we have seen before, a lonely salvation is not the ideal and does not make sense. The perfected individual is one with all. Loneliness can only be a stage, it is not an end. And loneliness need not separate, it may and often does unite as well.

"We miss the secret of the human birth if we do not see that each individual man is that Self and sums up all human potentiality in his own being. . . .No State or legislator or reformer can cut him rigorously into a perfect pattern; no Church or priest can give him a mechanical salvation, no order, no class life or ideal, no nation, no civilization or creed, or ethical, social or religious Shastra can be allowed to say to him permanently: On this way of mine and thus far shalt thou grow and act and in no other way." True, he has to use the ideals, disciplines, systems of co-operation which he finds in course of his search, or what others have found before him. But he can only use them well, if they are to him means towards something beyond them and not burdens to be borne for their own sake or despotic controls to be obeyed by him as their slave and subject.

The liberty claimed by the struggling human mind for the individual is no mere egoistic revolt and challenge, however egoistically and with whatever exaggeration it may have at times expressed itself. It is true the individual belongs not only to himself but also to society, the race, the national type, to humanity. But in a deeper view it is also true that he exceeds the human formula—that he belongs to God and to the world of all beings and to the godheads of the future. The free development of the individual and a respect for the same freedom in others would, therefore, seem to be the ideal law of social development which the imperfect human race has never yet fully attained and it may be very long before it can attain that, a real *consortium vitae, divini et humani juris communicatio.* Still it is this ideal, of free growth rather than a constructed growth by rule and limit, that has to be held up before the evolving individual.

The ideal group, the "beloved community", if it materializes, will not be brought about nor held together by any man-made rules and formulas, by what is called planning. The human mind cannot really foresee, much less lay down the law of this enormous transition or transformation. "What is a perfect technique of yoga, or rather of a world-changing or Nature-changing yoga?" Sri Aurobindo once asked in answer to a disciple's letter. "Not one that takes a man by a little bit of him somewhere, attaches a hook and pulls him up by a pulley into Nirvana or Paradise. The technique of a world-changing yoga has to be as multiform, sinuous, patient, all-including as the world itself. If it does not deal with all the difficulties or possibilities and carefully deal with each necessary element, has it any chance of success? And can a perfect technique which everyone can understand do that?"[18] In other words, the mystic groups would be institutions that would not be an institution at all or not that primarily. We who have supped full on the horror of Organization Man—indeed have known little else—and seen how Mechanization Has Taken Over may well wonder at the possibility of a free society of spiritual seekers, who could carry our effete and self-destroying civilization to an undreamt-of fulfillment. But "the evolved man has reached a state of development of his conscience which enables him to broaden his outlook and to become fully aware of the magnificent role he can play as a responsible actor in Evolution. Unlike the polyp who blindly fights for his life at the bottom of the sea and will never know that he is laying the foundation of a coral atoll which, in the course of centuries, will become a fertile island swarming with higher forms of life, man knows that he is the forerunner of a finer and more perfect race which will be partly his doing. He should be proud of the tremendous responsibility bestowed upon him, and his pride should be great enough to overshadow the inevitable but momentary disappointments and hardships. If only more people could grasp this, if they gloried in their work, if they rejoiced in it, the world would soon become a better world, long before the spiritual goal is reached."[19]

Such is the faith of the mystics. In that faith they will triumph. There are difficulties but, if we know how to look at them, difficulties are also opportunities. In any case they have never held back men from trying. The thing shall be done by the doing, the hope of an ideal group or society, a fairer world in which the spiritual life would be the normal life and not, as now, something to be striven for or imposed upon the rest. Here is a way out, if there is one anywhere, out of the impasse of history. This will be other than the compulsive or fixed ways of religious orders and societies. As Waite (*Lamps of Western Mysticism*) has said, other ways are possible. Yes, other tried and untried ways of the spirit. Perhaps it will be less an old-type monastery and more like an ashram, where all are welcome, according to their need and capacity and which has no rigid, sectarian rules to observe. Or it will be the spirit of the old doorkeeper who told Tolstoy who had knocked for rest and refuge: We receive everyone. While that is the ideal, unideal difficulties are within the range of possiblity too. Maybe "we have to face the tragedy that the whole situation of modern man is so far out of hand that we shall be compelled to let external events take their terrible course. In this case the only hope left will be the withdrawal of a remnant into a temporary solitude of the spirit, there to derive power from the only source which can in the long run change human life for the better."[20] But whatever happens, "there is in all of us a margin of initiative."[21]

How or what shall we choose? Perhaps our enlightened moderns will need, first of all, a dose of humility to cure themselves of their entrenched folly. In this respect the older cultures seem to be better off, if only they can throw off their form-fetishism, because they still have "the memory of men who trained themselves by silence and solitude and reading and meditation and so came to a knowledge superior to that of the multitude engrossed in fighting and bargaining. . . . The wise men fitted into these societies, whereas he seems out of place in a society which will not go beyond a common or 'horse' sense."

The journey is long. But, as the old Chinese saying has it, the journey of a thousand *li-s* begins with a step. We can always take that step, we who have been moving on that onward journey from the beginning of history. Even today there are indications on the horizon, not one but many:

"Purity of heart, too, is the beginning of the monk's union with his brothers. His true union: for monastic charity is not merely a 'social contract', a bargain arrived at by the agreement of many egoisms. It is the purity of heart which is reached only when the separate wills of the brethren become one will, the one will, the will of Christ. This community of will cannot be attained by a business-deal. It is an embrace of souls in the purity of the Spirit of God . . .the fulfilment of the Eucharistic mystery which is the heart of the monastic life.

"But when will such fulfilment be realized? Can it be attained perfectly on this earth? Who can say? . . .But they are at least beginning on earth to build a heavenly city."[22]

The heavenly city is not yet built, but it is forever building.[23]

"We seek. That is a fact. We seek a city still out of sight. In the contrast with the goal we live. But if this be so, then already we possess something of Being even in our finite seeking. For the readiness to seek is already something of an attainment, even if a poor one."[24]

It only asks a little of us here.
It asks of us a certain height.

VII

The Prospects Today

". . .the horror resides in the failure to enlist all those who swing the pick in the community of mankind.
—*Saint-Exupery*

A few statements, old and new, will show:

"Modern man begins to see that every step in material 'progress' adds just so much force to the threat of a more stupendous catastrophe."
—Carl Jung, *Modern Man in Search of a Soul*

"Shall we then sin, that grace may abound?"   —Bible

"The old order is over anyhow."
—Gerald Heard

'Do you not hear the entrance of a new theme?"   —Cecil Day Lewis

"O Lord, this is not the work of one day nor
children's sport."   —*Imitation of Christ*

"The way is all so very plain that we may
lose the way."   —G. K. Chesterton

So, where do we stand today, and where do we go from
here? and how does mysticism come in?

We stand, at last, trembling and tottering, on the edge
of the Abyss, and if we do not choose wisely we may, as
many fear, go under. This is no rhetorical threat, such as
prophets of doom delight to deliver. The Western world is
tottering under the onslaughts of forces of destruction it
was harboring as its most treasured possession. Our
civilization is challenged by its own offspring. Maybe
when the strong have devoured each other—perhaps it
would not be so bad if they devoured only each other and
left the others—the mystics shall inherit the earth. How
much better if that could happen before the Disaster, and
the costly education be avoided! Whatever happens, the
mystics have always pointed to the necessity of choice, if
we are to go ahead or even survive, the choice that might
provide the necesary breakthrough. It will never be an
easy thing, even if we agree to follow them, which is not
certain. Nearly everything in our modern society seems
opposed to it. To accept the mystic insight and activity
would mean a radical change of nearly every idea and institution responsible for the present phase of our civilization—or decivilization, as some would like to call it.
Maybe the hour has come, as William James said, when
mysticism must be faced in good earnest.

Going back in history one remembers what Hume
wrote, with characteristic self-assurance: "If we take in
our hand any volume, of divinity or school metaphysics,
for instance, let us ask, Does it contain any abstract
reasoning concerning quantity and number? No. Does it

contain any experimental reasoning concerning matter of fact or evidence? No. Commit it then to the flames, for it can contain nothing but sophistry and illusion." In the light of a larger knowledge his own book would be perhaps the first to qualify for that singular honor. As Sorokin points out: "We have seen that modern sensate culture emerged with a major belief that true reality and true value were mainly or exclusively sensory. Anything that was supersensory was either doubtful as a reality, or, being imperceivable by the senses, amounted to the non-existent....Its first positive fruit is an unprecedented development of the natural sciences and technological inventions. The first poisonous fruit is a fatal narrowing of the realm of true reality and true value."[1] It is this "fatal narrowing" that has led many of our thinkers and artists, guilty, uneasy and afraid, openly or by indirection towards the Mystic Way. Some have been apprehensive of spelling it clearly lest it sound too unorthodox or un-"scientific", while others have not hesitated to announce their affiliation, discovery, or rediscovery. Dean Inge, for instance: "I am venturing to predict," he wrote, "a revival of spiritual or otherworldly religion....I have this opinion partly on the tendency of human nature to seek for compensations. Now that the idols ... are lying broken at the foot of the pedestals; now that ... the last western heresy, the belief in an automatic law of progress, has been so far disproved ... that it has become a manifest absurdity; now that we are losing faith in our political institutions, it is plain that we must either give up hope ... or once more fix our hearts where true joys are to be found....If, as I believe, we are threatened not with another Dark Age, but with a period of contracting civilization, we are likely to see a revival of community life, and perhaps another flowering time of mysticism and mystical religion....If I am right, if we may look for a rebirth of spiritual religion,

we must expect, as in former revivals, it will be very independent of the Churches, and not too kindly regarded
by the ecclesiastics."² Such opinions are gaining ground,
within and without the churches. The voice of wisdom has
always been heard above the mêlée. Here it is, once
again, from Sri Aurobindo:

"At present mankind is undergoing an evolutionary
crisis in which is concealed a choice of its destiny, for a
stage has been reached in which the human mind has
achieved in certain directions an enormous development
while in others it stands arrested and bewildered and can
no longer find its way. A structure of the external life has
been raised up by man's ever-active mind and life-will, a
structure of an unmanageable hugeness and complexity,
for the service of his mental, vital, physical claims and
urges, a complex political, social, administrative,
economic, cultural machinery, an organised collective
means for his intellectual, sensational, aesthetic and
material satisfaction. Man has created a system of
civilisation which has become too big for his limited mental capacity and understanding and his still more limited
spiritual and moral capacity to utilise and manage, a too
dangerous servant of his blundering ego and its appetites.
For no greater seeing mind, no intuitive soul of knowledge
has yet come to his surface of consciousness which could
make this basic fullness of life a condition for the free
growth of something that exceeded it. . . .It is being used
instead for the multiplication of new wants and an aggressive expansion of the collective ego. At the same time
Science has put at his disposal many potencies of the
universal Force and has made the life of humanity
materially one; but what uses this universal Force is a little human individual or communal ego with nothing
universal in its light of knowledge or its movements, no inner sense or power which would create in this physical
drawing together of the human world a true life unity, a

111

mental unity or a spiritual oneness. All that is there is a chaos of clashing mental ideas, urges of individual and collective physical want and need, vital claims and desires, impulses of an ignorant life-push, hungers and calls for life satisfaction of individuals, classes, nations, a rich fungus of political and social and economic nostrums and notions, a hustling medley of slogans and panaceas for which men are ready to oppress and be oppressed, to kill and be killed, to impose them somehow or other by the immense and too formidable means placed at his disposal, in the belief that this is his way out to something. . . .But because the burden which is being laid on mankind is too great for the present littleness of the human personality and its petty mind and small life-instincts, because it cannot operate the needed change, because it is using this new apparatus and organisation to serve the old infra-spiritual and infra-rational life-self of humanity, the destiny of the race seems to be heading dangerously, as if impatiently and in spite of itself, under the drive of the vital ego seized by colossal forces which are on the same scale as the huge mechanical organisation of life and scientific knowledge which it has evolved, a scale too large for its reason and will to handle, into a prolonged confusion and perilous crisis and darkness of violent shifting incertitude. Even if this turns out to be a passing phase or appearance and a tolerable structural accommodation is found which will enable mankind to proceed less catastrophically on its uncertain journey, this can only be a respite. For the problem is fundamental and in putting its evolutionary Nature in man is confronting herself with a critical choice which must one day be solved in the true sense if the race is to arrive or even to survive."[3]

An informed, integral mysticism could be the overall answer to all this, a way out of the impasse. "A life of unity, mutuality and harmony born of a deeper and wider truth of our being" is the hope, for which the mature mystics have stood. This will be the Universal or Invisible Church of those that know, "the unifying of history" for which we have been waiting and which this age, if it so wills, might make possible. This will not be done by any get-together of ecumenical councils to settle ancient theological disputes. The world and not any accredited church, or number of churches, the united or disunited nations, is the mystical body of God. But the details of transition may well be left on the knees of the gods, if they have any use for an erring human race.

"From the integralist standpoint, the present antagonism between science, religion, philosophy, ethics and art is unnecessary, not to mention disastrous. In the light of an adequate theory of true reality and purpose, they all are one, and all serve one true purpose: the unfolding of the Absolute in the relative empirical world, to the greater nobility of Man and to the greater glory of God. As such they should and can co-operate in the fulfilment of this greatest task. . . .Our remedy demands a complete change of the contemporary mentality, a fundamental transformation of our system of values, and the profoundest modification of our conduct toward other men, cultural values, and the world at large."[4] To the eye of faith: "Therefore the time grows ripe and the tendency of the world moves toward a new and comprehensive affirmation in thought and in inner and outer experience and to its corollary, a new and rich self-fulfilment for the race."

This, one might say, is the theory or expectation. But it is obvious that there will be many problems of transition likely to wreck the plan, failures that would be a sore trial to the faithful. So while we must not look for any short cut, indeed must anticipate a long, even endless labor of adjustment and renewal, this will be a much better thing than to acquiesce in the existing evil or wait for an inglorious exit which is all that the present dispensation promises and so liberally distributes every now and then.

If, apparently, no age has been more removed than ours from such an attitude or approach as we have tried to outline, none needs it so much. In fact, we are loud in opposing it. But in most traditional views hostility to truth is a recognized technique and difficulties have been termed opportunities. This unspiritual age of ours, at least based on unspiritual foundations, calls for its opposites. The dread message of the Atom Bomb (the *ne plus ultra* of separation and slaughter), calls for a counteraction by the deathless Atman (the ultimate spiritual principal of unity and interrelation on which mysticism depends). In the words of our most sensitive historical thinker: "The release of atomic energy by Western technology in A.D. 1945 has had three effects on the Western technician's position. After having been undeservedly idolized, for a quarter of millennium, as the good genius of Mankind, he has suddenly found himself undeservedly execrated, as an evil genius who has released from his bottle a jinni that may perhaps destroy human life on Earth. The arbitrary change in the technician's fortunes is a severe ordeal, but his loss of popularity has not hit him so hard as his loss of confidence in himself. Till 1945 he believed, without a doubt, that the results of his work were wholly beneficent. Since 1945 he has begun to wonder whether his professional success may not have been a social and moral disaster."[5] Earlier, in *Modern Man in Search of a Soul*, Jung had told us of the working of the law of psychic compensation, how while the champions of the French Revolution were celebrating the worship of the Goddess of Reason (very appropriately, one might add, impersonated by a lady from the streets, *une fille de joie*) the West had also received its first translation of the *Upanishads*. "I cannot take it as an accident," says Jung, "it seems to me rather to satisfy a psychological law whose validity in personal life, at least, is complete. . . .No psychic value can disappear without being replaced by another of equivalent intensity. . . .Du Perron) brought the Eastern mind to the West, and its influence upon us we cannot yet measure. Let us beware of underestimating it."

In our present crisis too, the Decline of the West which engulfs us all, the star may rise in the East, the East being the land where the Sun rises. What Father Zossima, in *The Brothers Karamazov*, says about the east is true of the mystics, for they are always turned towards it. "And when the time comes, they will show it to the tottering creeds of the world. . . .That is the great thought. The star will rise out of the East." That is why we have now and then used the insight of an eastern sage too little known for his importance. But this implies no idolatry of place, person, or geography. The East, or the Sun, is a symbol and not a physical object. To talk in terms of division and differences even here can but be a continuing folly. It is a common crisis and the resources of mysticism everywhere are needed for all alike. Maybe in the process mysticism itself will shed some of its historical forms, its excesses and accidents and acquire a new look. In this respect those venerable elders—not a few—who are still trying to perpetuate the dying gospel of separation between peoples, are perhaps not acting in the best interest of the cause. As someone has said, it is strange how the Devil has invaded the realm of mystical theology and shares the ground about equally with God. To set, for instance, the mysticisms of the East and the West at variance is to carry over from an earlier, false feud; it is to prolong that "blandly bumptious provincialism" which has today little or no right to exist. To say, as Denis de Rougement and Henri Massis have done, that Eastern mysticism is unacceptable, or, as Zaehner has done even more openly, that it is a heresy is not likely to endear them to lovers of truth. In one of his earlier essays T. E. Eliot had informed us that "a spirit of excessive tolerance is to be deprecated." Indeed, for how else can we appreciate the strength of his own suggestion? It is sad to see even Maritain falling for these futile and false distinctions, between what he calls natural experience and supernatural experience. Most revealing, in this context, is Sadhu Sunder Singh's neat reflection on such dogmatists: "very nice but very narrow." Simone Weil, who was no church theologian, saw into the truth more clearly than those with this more-holy-than-thou complex. "It is necessary," she said, "that differences should not decrease friendship and that friendship likewise should not decrease difference." Behold, how they love one another, said the pagans about the early Christians. How one wishes the same could be said about the self-styled mystics. Perhaps the mystics know the truth all right, it is the narrow-minded pundits, the intellectuals and the ecclesiastics, who fail in the final test, whose pride and puerility prevent them from recognizing the simple truth of unity in diversity. As Krishna said, it is only children that make distinctions. The great mystics have preferred to echo the poet's tongue: "O world, I cannot hold you close enough!" To the agent of division they would say, with one voice, Nescio te, I know you not. How much more tolerant, in this respect, has been the attitude of the eastern texts! Toynbee, who is never weary of drawing Christian conclusions for the disasters of our times, has rightly recognized the exemplary tradition of toleration that has marked eastern and Hindu mysticism. 'The demand that one's religious sentiment be comprehensive makes for tolerence. One knows that one's life alone does not contain all possible values or all facets of meaning. Other people too have their stake in truth. The religion of maturity makes the affirmation God is, but only the religion of immaturity will insist, God is precisely what I say He is. The Hindu Vedas were speaking mature language when they asserted, 'Truth is one, men call it by many names'." In the words of Kabir: "Benares is to the East, Mecca to the West, but explore your heart, there is both Ram and Allah." Or, to quote the Persian sufi:

> My heart has become capable of every form;
>   it is a pasture for gazelles and a
>   convent for Christian monks;
> And a temple for idols, and the pilgrim's
>   Ka'ba and the table of Torah and
>   the book of the Koran.
> I follow the religion of love,
>   whichever way his camels take.

This is the universal and non-denominational form of mysticism, the most likely form of the world religion to be. Factionalism, such as exists, will have to go, those cherished dogmas of the schools will have to go, before the truth which demands our total loyalty. The deeper one probes into the psyche the less is one bothered by these man-made differences. The differences exist, but to insist on them and them alone, is to fail to see the sense of their existence, it is to declare oneself as immature. For these are not differences that divide, but "sweet difference of the Same." In true mystical experience, "East and West and other differences vanish."

That "East and West and other differences" have not vanished but multiplied is due to several reasons. Behind the present crisis stands the false image of Man and Reality created by the latest faith known as Science, ably aided by industrialism, commercial advertisement, periodic wars, and nationalistic jealousies. Across the sad centuries the words of *Chhandogya Upanishad* haunt us: "Whoever follows this false picture of the Self must perish." Alexis Carrel brings the same evidence and the same judgment: "Modern civilization finds itself in a difficult position because it does not suit us. It has been

117

created without any knowledge of our real nature....These theories build up civilizations which although designed for man fit only an incomplete monstrous image of man....In truth, our civilization...has created conditions of existence which...render life impossible." It is hard to disagree. In *The Measure of Man,* Joseph Wood Krutch hit the nail on the head: "How defective, therefore, is that so-called Science of Man which never really asks the questions at all and thus proves itself to be not the Science of Man, but only the Science-Of-What-Man-Would-Be-Like-If-He-Were-Not-a-Man-But-a-Machine." The error would seem to lie in what Whitehead called a bifurcation of nature. The whole thing is due to a confusion of concepts, due to the simple fact that our physicists and mathematicians have applied to man concepts that belong to the mechanical world. As a result "the sciences of inert matter have led us into a country that is not ours." It is not the claims of the mystics but of incomplete scientists that are "intolerably arrogant" and mistaken. Prodigals of perversity, the only way for us to get back home—to the Fatherland, as Plotinus called it— is the Mystic Way, of self-discovery. In this we are not being asked to forego "the blessings of science" but only to take the fangs out of her folly. As we have insisted throughout, mysticism itself is a kind of science, the science of the Whole. "Oh, taste, and see," cried one of the early modern mystic initiates, "here we are, a small family. . . .Yet one that refuses to die out. . . .You will find it impossible to prove that the world as seen by the mystics is less real than that which is expounded by science." The spirit and technique of science are our precious and hard-won possessions. But these can no longer blind us to the obvious and dangerous limitations of the scientific picture of the universe, or what is presented to us as the scientific picture. To mention only one. Dazzled by statistics and the impersonal methods of scientific inquiry, modern society ignores the individual. It believes only in the reality of the Universal and the impersonal. Man has become "abstracted" from the universe, to which present-day social and political methods offer exact parallels. Ours is a mass culture in which the individual is lost. It was Hitler's boast that his party would "socialize the soul" of man. In the Soviet Union unpopular individuals and groups are, from time to time, scientifically "liquidated." Long live science!

The results of such unethical, mistaken views of man and life are there for all to see. And yet so deep-seated is the habit of mechanical reliance—*Om Mani Padme Science*—and so blinding the triumphs of Know-How that "it will be difficult to get rid of a doctrine which, during more than three hundred years, has dominated the intelligence of the civilized world. The majority of men of science believe in the reality of Universals, the exclusive right of existence of the quantitative, the supremacy of Matter, the separation of the mind from the body, and the subordinate position of the mind. They will not easily give up this faith. For such a change would shake pedagogy, medicine, hygiene, psychology and sociology to their foundations. . . .It is obvious that the liberation of man from the materialistic creed would transform most of the aspects of our existence. . . .Therefore modern society will oppose with all its might this progress in our conceptions." Even if the alternative is, as it must be, total ruin.

From his mystical and pacifist point of view this is what Aldous Huxley had to say: "Recent scientific investigation has made it clear that the world of sense experience and of common sense is only a small part of the world as a whole. . . .What are the general conclusions to be drawn from the scientific picture of life's history on this planet?" The conclusions would seem to be that the picture is incomplete. To trust this picture as the whole truth can but add to our trouble.

"No account of the scientific picture of the world would be complete unless it contained a reminder of the fact, frequently forgotten by the scientists themselves, that this picture does not even claim to be comprehensive. From the world we actually live in, the world that is given by our senses, our intuitions of beauty and goodness, our emotions and impulses, our moods and sentiments, the man of science abstracts a simplified private universe of things possessing only those qualities which used to be called 'primary'. . . .By using the technique of simplification and abstraction, the scientist has succeeded to an astonishing degree in understanding and dominating the physical environment. The success was intoxicating and with an illogicality which, in the circumstances, was doubtless pardonable, many scientists and philosophers came to imagine that this useful abstraction from reality was reality itself. Reality as actually experienced contains intuitions of value and significance, contains love, beauty, mystical ecstasy, intimations of Godhead.

"Science did not and still does not possess intellectual instruments with which to deal with these aspects of reality. Consequently it ignored them. This has led to the error of identifying the world of science, a world from which all meaning and value has been deliberately excluded, with ultimate reality."

The process of identifying an arbitrary abstraction from reality with reality itself has been well described by Burtt in his *Metaphysical Foundations of Modern Science*. In Burtt's words:

"The founders of the philosophy of science were mathematical pragmatists, of a rather extreme type. They were absorbed in the mathematical study of nature. Metaphysics they tended to avoid, so far as they could; so far as not, it became an instrument for further mathematical conquest of the world. . . .With final causes and secondary qualities banished from the world of science it did not much matter how rough their subsequent treatment. . . .Hence if they be proved clearly false, it is important to do away with these guilty mathematical pretensions. It may be that a heavy and discouraging incubus will be thrown off just by the recognition of the fact."

The dangers of not doing so are today sufficiently real. In the words of a modern mystic whose insight we have had occasion to use before: "The modern spirit has found another light, the light of Science. . . the economic, social ultimate—an ideal, material organisation of civilisation and comfort, the use of reason and science and education for the generalisation of a utilitarian rationality which will make the individual a perfected social being in a perfected economic society. . . .(But) this ideal, this conscious reversion to the first state of man, his early barbaric state and its pre-occupation with life and matter, is a spiritual retrogression with the resources of the mind of a developed humanity and a fully evolved science at its disposal. As an element in the total complexity of human life this stress on a perfected economic and material existence has its place in the whole: as a sole or predominant stress it is for humanity itself, for the evolution itself full of danger. The first danger is the resurgence of the old vital and material primitive barbarian in a civilised form; the means that Science has put at our disposal eliminates the peril of subversion and destruction of an effete civilisation by a stronger primitive people. But it is the resurgence of the barbarian in ourselves, in civilised man, that is the peril, and this we see all around us. For that is bound to come if there is no high or strenuous mental and moral ideal controlling and uplifting the vital and physical man in us and no spiritual ideal liberating him from himself into his inner being. Even if this relapse is escaped, there is another danger,—for the cessation of the evolutionary urge, a crystallisation into a stable comfortable mechanised social living without ideal or outlook is another possible outcome.[6] Reason cannot by itself long maintain the race in its progress; it can do so only if it is a mediator between the life and body and something higher and greater within him; for it is the inner spiritual necessity, the push from what there is yet unrealised within him that maintains in him, once he has attained to mind, the evolutionary stress, the spiritual nisus. That renounced, he must either relapse and begin all over again or disappear like other forms of life before him as an evolutionary failure, through incapacity to maintain or serve the evolutionary urge. At the best he will remain arrested in some kind of mediary typal perfection, like other animal kinds, while Nature pursues her way beyond him to a greater creation."[7]

Yet the prospects are not quite hopeless. The very opposition of science to the spirit admits of a different use and intention. In a letter to a disciple Sri Aurobindo once wrote: "The condition of present-day civilisation, materialistic with an externalised intellect and life-endeavour, which you find so painful, is an episode, but one which was perhaps inevitable. For if the spiritualisation of the mind, life and body is the thing to be achieved, the conscious presence of the Spirit even in the physical consciousness and material body, an age which puts Matter and the physical life in the forefront and devotes itself to the effort of the intellect to discover the truth of material existence, had perhaps to come. On one side, by materialising everything up to the intellect itself, it has created the extreme difficulty of which you speak. . .but, on the other hand, it has given the life in Matter an importance which the spirituality of the past was inclined to deny to it. In a way it has made the spiritualisation of it a necessity for spiritual seeking. . . .More than that we cannot claim for it; its conscious effect has been rather to stifle and almost extinguish the spiritual element in humanity, it is only by the divine use of the pressure of contraries and an intervention from above that there will be the spiritual outcome."[8]

Here we seem to touch upon the root of the matter, or one of the roots—the role of reason in man and history. Behind both the triumphs and terrors of Sciences stands this new Demiurge. What is its true function and how has it deviated from that? What is its relation with the life of the spirit? A triumph of individual intelligence, it now seems about to be engulfed in a collective collapse, largely its own doing. Let us trace the process, briefly, an inevitable process as it would seem.

We may quote Sri Aurobindo again: "Speculative and scientific reason for their means, the pursuit of a practicable social justice and sound utility for their spirit, the progressive nations of Europe set out on their search for this light and this law....It has been the fulfillment and triumph of the individualistic age of human society, it has seemed likely also to be its end, the cause of the death of individualism and its putting away and burial among the monuments of the past[9]....For this discovery by individual free-thought of universal laws of which the individual is almost a by-product...seems to lead logically to the supression of that very individual freedom which made the discovery and the attempt at all possible. . . .The result to which this points and to which it still seems irresistibly to be driving us is a new ordering of society by a rigid economic or governmental Socialism in which the individual must have his whole life and action determined for him at every step and in every point from birth to old age by the well-ordered mechanism of the State.

"But, most important of all, the individualistic age... has fixed two important ideas: the first is the democratic conception of the individual and secondly that the individual is not merely a social unit, not merely a member of a pack, hive or anti-hill; he is something in himself. That is an idea which agrees in its root with the profoundest and highest spiritual conception and has a part to play in the moulding of the future."

"Reason," continues the same authority, "is undoubtedly the highest developed faculty of man at his present stage of development. . . .Recently, however, there has been a very noticeable revolt of the human reason against the sovereignty of the intellect, a dissatisfaction of the reason with itself and its own limitations. The sovereignty has been always indeed imperfect, in fact a troubled, struggling, resisted and often defeated rule. . . .The highest power of reason, because its pure and characteristic power, is the disinterested seeking after true knowledge. When knowledge is pursued for its own sake, then alone are we likely to arrive at true knowledge. . . .But if from the beginning we have only particular ends in view, then we limit our intellectual gain. It is so indeed that the ordinary man uses his reason. . . .But even the man who is capable of governing his life by ideas is often not capable of the highest, the freest and disinterested use of this rational mind. As others are subject to the tyranny of other interests, prejudices, instincts or passions, so he is subjected to the tyranny of ideas. But the ideas themselves are partial and insufficient; not only have they only a very partial triumph, but if their success were complete, it would still disappoint, because they are not the whole truth of life. . . ."

This is the cause, or one of the causes, why all systems have failed, and deserved to fail, because their triumph would be the triumph of an imperfection. In the light of a reason more right than reason we can see that "the whole difficulty of the reason. . .is that because of its own inherent limitation it is unable to deal with life in its complexity. . .; it is compelled to break it up into parts. . .to work out a selection. . . .It would almost appear that there are two worlds, the world of ideas and the world of life. . . .The reason struggling with life becomes either an empiric or a doctrinaire.

"Reason can indeed make itself a mere servant of life. . . .But this is obviously to abdicate its throne or highest office and to betray the hope with which man set forth on his journey. . . .On the other hand, when it attempts a higher action reason separates itself from life. . . .The idealist, the thinker, the philosopher, the poet and artist, even the moralist, all those who live much in ideas, when they come to grapple at close quarters with practical life, seem to find themselves something at a loss and are constantly defeated in their endeavour to govern life by their ideas. . . .Reduce your ideal into a system and it at once begins to fail; apply your general laws and fixed ideas systematically as the doctrinaire would do[10], and life very soon breaks through or writhes out of their hold or transforms your system, even while it nominally exists, into something the originator would not recognise and would repudiate perhaps as the very contradiction of the principles which he sought to eternise."[11]

Why should this be so? It is so because at the very basis of our life there is something on which the unaided intellect can never lay hold of. Though an important and indispensable instrument for the human evolution, the reason is not the only, not the highest power in man. Reason is a help, reason is a bar. That depends. It is part of the mystic awakening to the truths of other levels that "the rational or intellectual man is not the last and highest ideal of manhood, nor would a rational society be the last and highest expression of the possibilities of an aggregate human life. . . .The Spirit that manifests in man and dominates secretly the phases of his development, is greater and profounder than his intellect and drives towards a perfection that cannot be shut in by the arbitrary constructions of the human reason. . . .

"The truth is that upon which we are now insisting, that reason is in its nature an imperfect light with a large but still restricted mission and that once it applies itself to life and action it becomes subject to what it studies. . . .(Also) it can in its nature be used and has always been used to justify any idea, theory of life, system of society or government, ideal of individual or collective action to which the will of man attaches itself for the moment or through the centuries. . . .

"This truth is hidden from the rationalist because he is supported by two constant articles of faith, first that his own reason is right and the reason of others who differ from him is wrong, and secondly that whatever may be the present deficiencies of the human intellect, the collective human reason will eventually arrive at purity and be able to found human thought and life securely on a clear rational basis entirely satisfying to the intelligence."

But, as we have seen, "the reason cannot arrive at any final truth because it can neither get to the root of things nor embrace the totality of their secrets;[12] it deals with the finite, the separate, the limited aggregate, and has no measure for the all and the infinite. Nor can reason found a perfect life or a perfect society. A purely rational society could not come into being and, if it could be born, either could not live or would sterilise and petrify human existence."

This is because the "root powers" of life are either below or above, in fact both. Reason is only a mid-term, it is an instrument of mediation between the subconscious and the superconscious, and, at a certain stage of development, it can open itself to the higher yet unevolved powers of the Spirit.[13] This it has not always or obediently done. This is seen very clearly from its usual attitude towards all higher truth and especially its "close rival", that is faith or religion. "Faced with the phenomenon of the religious life (reason) is naturally apt to adopt one of two attitudes, both of them shallow in the extreme, hastily presumptuous and erroneous. Either it views the whole thing as a mass of superstition, a mystical nonsense, a farrago of ignorant barbaric survivals,—that was the extreme spirit of the rationalist now happily, though not dead, yet much weakened and almost moribund,—or it patronises religion, tries to explain its origin, to get rid of it by the process of explaining it away; or it labours gently or forcefully to reject or correct its superstitions, crudities, absurdities, to purify it into an abstract nothingness or persuade it to purify itself in the light of the reasoning intelligence; or it allows it a role, leaves it perhaps for the edification of the ignorant, admits its value as a moralising influence or its utility to the State for keeping the lower classes in order, even perhaps tries to invent that strange chimera, a rational religion."

All this a study of the history of religions will show. "But the attempt to root out the imperfect things from religion or to purge religion of elements necessary for its completeness because the forms are defective or obscure, without having the power to illuminate them from within or the patience to wait for their illumination from above or without replacing them by more luminous symbols, is not to purify but to pauperise."

This should not be made to mean that reason and spirit are forever opposed, that if you have one you cannot have the other. This is one of the persistent errors of the human mind[14] inordinately fond of exclusive assertions and attachments. The wiser spirits have known better. "Sir, I oppose not the rational to the spiritual," wrote Whitcote, "for spiritual is most rational." The relations of the spirit and the reason need not be, as they too often are in practice, hostile to each other or without any point of contact. "Religion itself need not adopt for its principle the formula 'I believe because it is impossible' or Pascal's 'I believe because it is absurd.' What is impossible or absurd to the unaided reason becomes real and right to the reason lifted beyond itself by the power of the spirit and irradiated by its light." Hume asked, ironically, "Have you ever seen a world created under your eyes—have you ever observed an act of creation of the world?" The answer, as suggested by the mystics is, "Yes, there are men who have done that." "That Lord made me his, when first he went about his work, at the birth of time, before his creation began. . . . I was there when he enclosed the sea within its confines, forbidding the waters to transgress their assigned limits, when he poised the foundations of the world. I was at his side, a master workman, my delight increasing with each day as I made play before him all the while; made play in this world of dust, with the sons of Adam for my playfellows. Listen to me, then, you that are my sons that follow, to your happiness, in the paths I show you; listen to the teaching that will make you wise, instead of turning away from it." Or St. John: "I have seen with my eyes, and my hands have touched." Vedāhametam, I have known.

Applied to society the unmitigated rationalist formula has led, as we have witnessed, to interesting, characteristic, and disturbing consequences. Beginning with an outburst of individual energy it has gradually moved towards state control or the pseudo-democratic falsehood of the dominance of a class or party over the rest. In the process both liberty and equality had to be given up or else make room for some form of organization. The only item that has lingered on is brotherhood or comradeship. But this can never be compulsive, without losing its character, its raison d'être. Here the method of totalitarian mystiques is unmistakable. It is a bitter and violent betrayal of all reason and common sense, "the same in Russia as in Fascist countries, so that to the eye of the outsider the deadly quarrel (between the two) seems to be a blood-feud of kinsmen fighting for the inheritance of their slaughtered parents—Democracy and the Age of Reason...." Communist threats may not be able to achieve their end, for if they did it would be *ave atque vale* to the life of the reason, not to speak of the spirit.

The "red" light is there and the danger is far from being over. Maybe, to more critical eyes, "The pressure of the State organization on the life of the individual has reached a point where it is ceasing to be tolerable." The thoroughgoing mechanization, the logical, Pavlovian end of the process, is dreaded by those who can see furthest and have still some regard left for freedom of the spirit. To such thinking it might seem that some form of spiritual anarchism, to use a much abused word and idea, a free equality founded upon willing cooperation without mammoth organizations or other forms of compulsion, might be the way out towards a better society, composed of "devoted individuals" or what the old Russians called Sobornost. But, of course, the method employed is not so important, provided we keep on ascending. It will really be a method of no method, for "no machinery invented by reason can perfect either the individual or the collective man; an inner change is needed in human nature, a change never to be effected except by the few. This is not certain; but in any case, if this is not the solution, then there is no solution, if this is not the way, then there is no way for mankind."

This résumé on the role of reason in man and society must give us pause. Its services must not be whittled down even if we are unable to accept its arrogant claim to dictate the whole truth of man. It had a purpose to serve, which we may put like this: "The temptation to live merely as highly complex animal and to treat the physical world as the ultimate reality and true end of life has always been present for millions of souls who lacked the means to try it. It may be hoped that this magnificent trial and failure, which has affected not the West alone, but the whole world, was necessary to get the temptation out of the human system, at least in some degree."[15] If it would act as a gentle purge it would be a blessing indeed.

The quarrel between reason and spirituality, however unnecessary, is one with a long history. But mysticism itself is a new organon of understanding, it is not merely, or essentially, a state of *raptus*. That is a stage, or indication. In any case, as McTaggart liked to say, a mysticism which ignored the claim of understanding would be doomed. "None ever went about to break logic, but in the end logic broke him." The only proviso being that the logic of physics is not the monolithic master of man, the whole man. As Dean Inge has it, the mystic has little interest in appealing to a faculty 'above reason', "if reason is used in the proper sense, as the logic of the whole personality." Those who still think in terms of the whole will sooner or later accept the mystic rationale, which opens a door or way without which man's long journey through the ages would lack both point and purpose and without which, today, there is nothing but doom ahead of the blundering human race.

Some other, perhaps less spectacular services of the mystical attitude to modern society would be in the fields of power and action. The problem of power, it has been well said, is insoluble except by the saint. St. Francis would have been incapable of discovering the ICBM or of using it either. Patanjali had warned against the lure of *siddhis* or spiritual powers. What would he have said about the scientific *siddhis* of today? The spirits that came to Yeats during his seances gave him not only metaphor but also the ethics of mysticism. For every step one took towards power, they said, one should take three steps towards charity, a lesson that has been totally lost upon the scientific wizards of today. No wonder power politics is recoiling like a boomerang and paying such rich dividends in anxiety and neurosis, the almost certain *néantisation* of man and his "rational" civilization. Perhaps there is "No Exit". Perhaps there will be few or none left to benefit from retrospective wisdom, none to recollect in tranquillity. Or, "At the time of the end shall the vision be?" Is our Anxiety an awareness of Freedom? *In extremis*.

Sometimes our politicians seem to be quite aware of the pressure of the mystic minority. After all it was this conflict—between Caesar and God—that led to the trial. "Our Lord said that the children of this world are wiser in their generation than the children of light. That explains why the wicked who walk in darkness have a truer instinct about the location of the universal light switch and the best way to throw it....And when the hour of darkness is at hand in the country, the first act of the powers of evil is invariably to throw the switch. They rage the cloisters. They turn the contemplatives out of their monasteries with loud speeches about the good of the state and contributing to the social need. No one is deceived very long by such speeches; those who make these not for a moment."[16] The mystics have been a perennial opposition to all humanistic schemes and methods of forcing men to be free. Their utility is not yet over.

Another vexed sector of modern life where the mystic attitude throws the modern mind into an introspective mood is with regard to action and the idea of usefulness to man and society. It purifies pragmatism of all its grossness. At some time or other, if not at all times, the mystics have been accused of being inactive and worthless. In some cases the charge may have been well-founded. But it cannot be used as a stick to beat all mystics with. For the best among them have been men and women of enormous activity, perhaps the only kind of activity that leaves no bitter residue behind. As J. B. Rhine points out: "The great hope is in that minority who know that, however useful. . .physical discoveries may be, they are not carrying man toward the kind of world to which he really aspires, and the good life he wants to live with his fellow men. Some few at least recognise the tragedy that, in this vast scientific conquest of physical nature, it is man himself that is being conquered. . . .They realise that not all of the most brilliant physical explorations put together, whether penetrating into the nuclear energies of the atom or reaching far out to the remotest galaxy, have brought man even a short step nearer to grasping the essential mystery of himself as a personality. They know, too, that there are other directions. . . .As a spark can start a conflagration, so can a handful of perceptive men and women initiate a movement they could not stop or even guide."[17] These things do not depend on number. "We are still at the dawn of human evolution, and if only one man out of a million were endowed with a conscience, this would suffice to prove that a new degree of liberty has appeared. Many important steps in the history of evolution started out as a mutation affecting only a very small number of individuals, perhaps only one."[18] Or, to quote Fosdick: "As a matter of fact, it is always the minorities that hold the key of progress. The still small voice speaking through the conscience of a man, bidding him choose obloquy and ostracism rather than conformity is, now and always, the hope of the race."[19]

> Lonely antagonists of destiny
> Who went down. . .before many spears.

What is often forgotten about mystical activity is that the mystics have always had a well-defined theory of action which spares them the stupid expenditure of all kinds of energy which has become a mark of an age without the slightest discrimination. As Aldous Huxley has shown, the practical mystics have critically examined the whole idea of action and have laid down, in regard to it, a set of rules, for the guidance of those desiring to follow the mystic path towards the beatific vision. Or, as Swami Pravabhananda says, summing up the Indian attitude, "Not *karma*, mere action, but *karma yoga*, union with God through action." Along with the classic doctrine of *nishkāma karma*, non-attached action, the mystics also know of liberated action, *muktasya karma*. "Liberation and transcendence need not necessarily impose a disappearance, a sheer dissolving out from the manifestation; it can prepare a liberation into action of the highest knowledge and an intensity of Power that can transform the world and fulfil the evolutionary urge."

But of course the mystics do not suffer from any dogooder complex. "They did not seek God *in order to* return to the world better fitted for active life."[20] Contrasted with their theory and practice, most of our well-laid schemes, apart from going 'aft agley', look puerile and part of the vicious circle. The idea of usefulness to humanity is surely one of the persistent errors of our times. Even Simone Weil had tried to expound the *Upanishads* to peasant girls and Greek mythologies to factory workers. Perhaps the mystics do even more good because of what they are, or become, than by what they do or say.

Many years ago a wise lady had been asked if yoga, which may be defined as the discipline of mysticism, was likely to benefit humanity. Yoga, she had answered, was for the sake of Divinity. It was not the welfare of humanity that was directly aimed at. Whether humanity as a whole would be benefited or not would depend on the condition of humanity itself. Humanity would have to change much before it could hope to profit from yoga or mysticism. How many desire that change may be doubted. But salvation is never a matter of statistics. What is important is that the thing should be done at all, in however small a number; that is the only difficulty. If this is not done, if even the small number is not there, if a new kind of sanctity fails to materialize, then indeed will mankind become a useless passion.

There will be neither United Nations nor One World unless we have united notions. Perhaps none can help us better in this task than the mystics. It will be a test for them as well. They alone have the know-how. In all times and ages they have spoken with the same voice, acted unwearily, without rest, without haste. The satire of their presence, to use Emerson's phrase about Thoreau, is meant to profit us. Or shall it be rather:

> Our fathers have been churchmen
> Nineteen hundred years or so,
> And to every new proposal
> They have always answered No!

For the good of the world, as well as out of self-respect, it is better to believe that there will always be a few whose supreme loyalty will be to a realm of meanings yet to be.[21] The few may still "save the city."

References and Notes

CHAPTER I

What It Is

1. *The Cloud of Unknowing*, the original work of this title by an unknown mystic, has been followed in recent years by a commentary of the same title by Ira Progoff. My reference here is to the original.
2. *Conference of the Birds*, Farid Ud-Din Attar.
3. *Summa Theologiae*, St. Thomas Aquinas.

CHAPTER II

The Situation

1. Arnold J. Toynbee, *An Historian's Approach to Religion*, Preface.
2. Jacques de Marquette, *Introduction to Comparative Mysticism*, 18.
3. Robert Alfred Vaughan, *Hours with the Mystics*, II, 356.
4. Samuel Rosenkranz, *The Meaning of Your Life*, 77.

5. Sri Aurobindo, *The Life Divine.*
6. C. D. Broad, *Religion, Philosophy and Psychical Research*, 172-73.
7. W. R. Inge, *Mysticism in Religion*, 137.
8. Alexis Carrel, *Man the Unknown*, 321.
9. Karl Jaspers, *The Future of Mankind*, 66, 154-55.
10. Lecomte du Noüy, *Human Destiny*, III, 251.
11. H. A. Overstreet, *The Mature Mind*, 119-20.
12. Sister Mary Francis, P.C., *A Right to be Merry*, 47.
13. Sri Aurobindo, in a letter to a disciple, wrote: "It is because people do not understand. . .or realise the significance of the emergence of consciousness in a world of inconscient Matter that they are unable to realise this inevitability. I suppose a matter-of-fact observer, if there had been one. . .would have criticised any promise of the emergence of life in a world of dead earth and rock and mineral as an absurdity and a chimera; so too afterwards he would have repeated this mistake and regarded the emergence of thought and reason in an animal world as an absurdity and a chimera. It is the same now with the appearance of the supermind in the stumbling mentality of this world of human consciousness and its reasoning ignorance." *On Yoga*, I, II, 14.

CHAPTER III

AN APPROACH

1. One of the earliest and well-known works on this subject concludes with the following not very bright but quite damaging observation: "It (mysticism) shall be called Bottom's dream, because it hath no bottom."—Vaughan, *Hours with the Mystics*, 1856. In more sober language, "Neither the word nor the thing is in good standing among us today."—C. A. Bennett, *A Philosophical Study of Mysticism*, 70. "Today," or was it "yesterday"? As Dean Inge pointed out, in *Christian Mysticism*: "The word mysticism has been almost always used in a slightly contemptuous sense in the nine-

teenth century. It was supposed to indicate something repugnant to the robust common sense and virile rationality of the British character." God bless the "virile rationality" of the British character!

2. As Stace has pointed out, "The very word 'mysticism' is an unfortunate one...better if we could use the words 'enlightenment' or 'illumination' which are commonly used in India." (*Mysticism and Philosophy*, 15.) This is quite true. "There is probably no more misused word in these our days than 'mysticism'." Dom Cuthbert Butler, *Western Mysticism*, 3.

3. Sri Aurobindo, *The Life Divine*, Ch. I. Also see W. R. Inge, *Christian Mysticism*, 5-6.

4. Swami Akhilananda, *Hindu Psychology*, 22.

5. Waite, *Lamps of Western Mysticism*, 243.

6. Evelyn Underhill, *Mysticism*, Preface.

7. Lecomte du Noüy, *Human Destiny*, 153.

8. Junayid.

9. Robert Alfred Vaughan, *Hours with the Mystics*, 27, xxxiii.

10. "The empire of illusion," Kant called it in a moment of uninspiration. The word "escape" or "flight" does not have a particularly happy association. But really it is not so simple, not a negation but a strategic movement of withdrawal. There are circumstances when "flight from the times is the only proper position" to take. Also, be it noted, there "are various kinds of escapism; the mystics are not the only culprits."—W. R. Inge, *Mysticism in Religion*, 146.

11. "Is there then an unbridgeable gulf between that which is beyond and that which is here or are they two perpetual opposites and only by leaving this adventure in Time behind, by overleaping the gulf can man reach the Eternal?... That is what seems to be at the end of one line of experience....But there is also this other and indubitable experience that the Divine is here in everything as well as above and behind everything....It is a significant and illuminating fact that the Knower of *Brahman* even moving and acting in this world, even bearing all its shocks, can live in some absolute peace, light and beatitude of the Divine. There is then here something other than that mere trenchant opposition—there is a mystery, a problem which one would think must admit of

some less desperate solution. This spiritual possibility points beyond itself and brings a ray of hope into the darkness of our fallen existence."—Sri Aurobindo, *On Yoga*, I, 25-6.

12. The mystic is never a peddler in petty reforms. But, as we shall see, his presence rouses resentment. On two grounds: first, self-respect causes us to regard such intrusion as an intolerable impertinence; secondly, the would-be reformer is guilty of impertinence. This is the observation of a philosophical critic, C. A. Bennett. It may be said, in defense, that no genuine mystic ever dreams of "intruding" or imposing his will on others. Sorokin, though he does not speak entirely from the mystical standpoint, is nearer the truth. "Our remedy demands a complete change of the contemporary mentality, a fundamental transformation of our system of values, and the profoundest modification of our conduct toward other men, cultural values, and the world at large." *The Crisis of Our Age*, 321. Again: For "a transformation of the mentality of Western culture" he does not believe in any "recommendation of purely mechanical, communistic or totalitarian 'socialization' and 'communization'....Such mechanical procedure can give only the same disastrous results for society as they have invariably given before....There must be a change of the whole mentality and attitude in the direction of the norms prescribed in the Sermon on the Mount. When such a change occurs, to a notable degree the technical ways of remodelling the economic and political structures in this direction become easy. Without this change, no mechanical, politico-economic reconstruction can give the desired results."—*Ibid.*, 319.

The distinction—or difference—between the two methods has been stated by Sri Aurobindo with his usual clarity and competence. "The churning of Matter by the...human intellect to conquer material Nature and use it for its purpose may break something of the passivity and inertia, but it is done for material ends, in a *rajasic* spirit, with a denial of spirituality as its mental basis. Such an attempt may end, seems to be ending indeed, in chaos and disintegration, while the new attempts at creation and reintegration seem to combine the obscure rigidity of material Nature with a resurgence of the barbaric brutality and violence of a half-animal vital Nature. How are the spiritual forces to deal with all that or make use of such a churning of the energies of the material universe? The way of the Spirit is the way of peace and light and harmony; if it has to battle, it is precisely because of the presence of such forces which seek either to extinguish or to prevent the spiritual light. . . .Materialism can hardly be spiritual in its basis, because its basic method is just the opposite of the spiritual way of doing things. The spiritual works from within outwards, the way of materialism is to work from out inwards. It makes the inner the result of the outer, fundamentally a phenomenon of Matter and it works upon that view of things. It seeks to 'perfect' humanity by outward means and one of its main efforts is to construct a perfect social machine which will train and oblige men to be what they ought to be. The loss of the ego in the Divine is the spiritual ideal; here it is replaced by the immolation of the individual to the military and industrial State. Where is there any spirituality in all that?" *On Yoga,* I, 8-9.

13. Sri Aurobindo, *The Life Divine.*
14. F. W. H. Myers, *Human Personality and Its Survival after Death,* 29.
15. *Grey Eminence.*
16. P. 15.
17. *Christian Behaviour,* 57.
18. The Mother, *Conversations,* 52-3.
19. A. N. Whitehead, *Function of Reason,* 8.
20. Eddington, *The Nature of the Physical World,* 334.
21. Rufus M. Jones, *The Eternal Gospel,* 159.
22. Rufus M. Jones, *Some Exponents of Mystical Religion,* 9.
23. Rufus M. Jones, *The Eternal Gospel.*
24. C. A. Bennett, *A Philosophical Study of Mysticism,* 163.
25. James Maynard Keynes.
26. *See:* "Man made the universe; he has made its nightmare, arbitrary quality (of polytheism), its inaccessible righteousness (monotheism), its blind, inhuman necessitarianism (of mechanism). Each of these has been a part picture of an aspect of his nature. He has only been able to see in outer

nature what confirms and answers to his inner nature. The invisible replies and rationalizes in the form in which it is summoned and imagined....

"As man dares act (this is the fact of creative faith) his apprehension-construction grows and he sees not subjectively but objectively a new reality. For he brings into being that which he has dared to desire." Gerald Heard, *The Third Morality*.

"The world is tired of individualism (which economic-dominated minds call by its economic symptom, capitalism).... The compulsory economic communism is based on hate. The psychological communism is based on love.... If the psychology is right, then the right economics, the only economics bearable...will follow." Gerald Heard, *The Social Substance of Religion*.

Again: "If evolution is to continue...it cannot continue unless we consciously co-operate with this, its next step, the evolution of consciousness, men who are forwarding that evolution must make for themselves not merely personal and private ways of life but also a new social pattern of living which permits and expresses their new type of consciousness....

"What then prevents intelligent people availing themselves of this way of deliverance? Nothing but the fact that society is, and must always be, based on psychology and have as its consequences and symptom of that psychology, an appropriate economics.... In fact, the reverse is true, that economics is basic and psychology the resultant.... We simply endure a diseased economics inevitably springing from an evil psychology....

"Only those who have discovered the path of evolution, what is the next step and how we are to co-operate with that development, can know themselves as part of a self-transcending purpose." Gerald Heard, *Sex, Pain and Time*.
27. Evelyn Underhill, *Practical Mysticism*, ix.
28. There has been too great a tendency, among a section of critics, to look upon the mystic as a lonely wolf, 'outsider' as the phrase is today. True, the great are always alone, but the simple fact is that the mystic is a pioneer of a new mutation,

engaged, as Colin Wilson has said, in the "creation of a higher type of man. . .with a broader consciousness and a deeper sense of purpose." "In the greatest mystics we see the highest and widest development of that consciousness to which the human race has yet attained. . . .The germ of that same transcendent life. . .is latent in all of us. . . ." Evelyn Underhill, *Mysticism*. Mysticism, as Alexis Carrel, himself a scientist, but a scientist with a broad vision, has pointed out, is among "the fundamental human activities."

29. ". . .they are like birds in the sky, placed on high, that is, in God, so that they know no limitation." Abbé Bremond, *La Conquete Mystique*.

CHAPTER IV

THE DOCTRINE OF THE MYSTICS

1. Dom Cuthbert Butler, *Western Mysticism*, 129.
2. Walter T. Stace, *Mysticism and Human Reason*, 25.
3. W. R. Inge, *Mysticism in Religion*, 152.
4. Rudolf Otto, *Mysticism, East and West*.
5. As regards "proof" of the existence of God: "To find or know God by any outward proofs, or by anything but God Himself, made manifest and self-evident in you will never be your case here or hereafter. . . .And all pretended knowledge of any of these things, beyond and without this self-evident sensibility of their birth within you, is only such knowledge of them as the blind man hath of the light that hath never entered into him." "*Jnānā* is eternal, is general, is necessary and is not a personal knowledge of this man or that man. It is there, as knowledge in the *Atman* itself, and lies there hidden under all *avidyā* (ignorance). . .unprovable, because self-evident, needing no proof, because itself giving to all proof the ground of possibility." *Ibid.*
6. According to Rudolf Otto, Eckhart established a "polar identity" between rest and motion, within the Godhead itself. *Mysticism, East and West*. Hume had said that it was im-

possible to *imagine* a self-contradictory state of affairs. But, then, the mystics don't imagine.

7. Alan W. Watts, *The Supreme Identity*.
   According to Royce, "The *Upanishads* contain already essentially the whole story of the mystic faith." *The World and the Individual*.

8. W. R. Inge, *Mysticism in Religion*, 29.

9. Pratt, *Religious Consciousness*, 366.

10. Binet, *Les Alterations de la Personalité*. *Also see* Charles H. Hinton, *An Episode in Flatland*; E. A. Abbot, *Flatland*, both of which show what human life, lived without many dimensions, would be like or is becoming like.

11. *The Life Divine*, 17-19.

12. Marquette, *Introduction to Comparative Mysticism*, 18.

13. Stace, *Mysticism and Human Reason*, 9.

14. Dorothy Berkeley Phillips, *The Choice Is Always Ours*, xxi.

15. The book was appropriately called *The Mind At The End Of Its Tether*. The entire mystic hypothesis is that there is something above and beyond the human reason.

16. J. B. Rhine, *New World of the Mind*, 212.

17. "They who see but One in all the changing manifoldness of the universe, unto them belongs Eternal Truth—unto none else, unto none else." *Upanishads*.
    "All things are one." Heraclitus, *Fragments*.
    As a result of his "experimental mysticism", as he calls it, Ouspensky found out: "This idea of unity of everything in whatever sense and on whatever scale it be taken, occupied a very important place in the conception of the world and of life that was formed in me in these strange states of consciousness....We are accustomed to take things as separate. Here there was nothing separate....I felt that the separate existence of anything—including myself—was a fiction, something non-existent, impossible." *A New Model of the Universe*.

18. Sri Aurobindo, *Hymns to the Mystic Fire*, pp. VI-VII, XII-XIII, XXIX-XXXII, XLVI-XLVII.

19. Lecomte du Noüy, *Human Destiny*.

CHAPTER V

THE ROLE OF THE INDIVIDUAL

1. Eastbrooks and Gross, *The Future of the Human Mind*, 233.
2. Sri Aurobindo, *The Life Divine*, 37.
3. *Ibid.*, 42-3.
4. Gordon W. Allport, *The Individual and his Religion*, 8.
5. Swami Vivekananda, *Works*, II, 13.
6. Sri Aurobindo, *On Yoga*, I, 4.
7. Sri Aurobindo, *the Life Divine*, 63.
8. Quoted in Godfrey Higgins, *Anacalypsis*, II, 430.
9. P. D. Ouspensky, *The Psychology of Man's Possible Evolution*.
10. Samuel Rosenkranz, *The Meaning of Your Life*, 75.
11. William James, *Varieties of Religious Experience*, 378-79.
12. Gardner Murphy, *Challenge of Psychical Research*, 287.
13. Fritz Kunkel and Roy E. Dickinson, *How Character Develops*.
14. D. T. Suzuki, *Zen Buddhism*, Anchor Books, 105.
15. J. B. Rhine, *New Worlds of the Mind*, 263-64.
16. Lancelot Law Whyte, *Accent on Form*, 191-92.
17. Sri Aurobindo, *The Life Divine*, 40.
18. Sri Aurobindo, *On Yoga*, I, 48.
19. Colin Wilson, *Religion and the Rebel*, 321.
20. *The Life Divine*.
21. "He is an Outsider because he stands for Truth." Colin Wilson, *The Outsider*, 13. What a commentary on the community, the Pillars of Society!
22. *The Life Divine*.
23. *Ibid.*
24. Hocking, *The Meaning of God in Human Experience*, 403-04.
25. C. A. Bennett, *A Philosophical Study of Mysticism*, 190.
26. Dom Cuthbert Butler, *Western Mysticism*, 136.
27. C. A. Bennett, *op. cit.*

CHAPTER VI

THE IDEAL GROUP

1. But, the suspicion is recurrent, among Mr. Wilson's ideal figures many are but a variation of the Underdog. The closeness should not surprise. Maybe "because civilization has created the Underdog and is creating more of his sort every day, and when it describes him it is looking in the mirror. You need only think for a moment of the men who are furthest away from him in everything that matters to realize that society is never likely to go the whole hog in working for mental, spiritual and physical balance. . . .The Romany gipsy and the saint came nearest to being in possession of their own souls. Civilization outlaws the one and still martyrs the other." Philip Toynbee (ed.) *Underdogs: Anguish and Anxiety*, 255.
2. C. A. Bennett, *A Philosophical Study of Mysticism*.
3. Rufus M. Jones, *The Eternal Gospel*, 184.
4. Lecomte du Noüy, *Human Destiny*, 109.
5. Sri Aurobindo, *On Yoga*, I, 3.
6. Gerald Heard, *The Human Venture*, 270-71.
7. Let one example suffice: "The Anaesthetic Revelation is the Invitation of Man into an Immemorial Mystery of the Open Secret of Being, revealed as the inevitable Vortex of Continuity", revealed through heroin, marijuana, mescalin, happiness pills and others to follow. O Brave New World, that has such addicts of the Absolute in it! O Transcendence without tears! *See also* P. D. Ouspensky's *A New Model of the Universe*, chapter on "Experimental Mysticism".
8. Aldous Huxley, *The Perennial Philosophy*, 43: "The saint is one who knows that every moment of our human life is a moment of crisis."
9. Colin Wilson, *Religion and the Rebel*, 320.
11. Aldous Huxley, *Ends and Means*, 147.
12. Rufus M. Jones, *Some Exponents of Mystical Religion*, 41.
13. Gordon W. Allport, *The Individual and His Religion*, 142.
14. Walter Nigg, *Warriors of God*, 16-18.
15. Carl Jung, *Modern Man In Search of a Soul*.

16. W. R. Inge, *Mysticism in Religion,* 16.
17. Sri Aurobindo, *The Human Cycle,* 279-80.
18. Sri Aurobindo, *On Yoga,* I, 14.
19. Lecomte du Noüy, *Human Destiny,* 273.
20. Alan W. Watts, *The Supreme Identity,* 39.
21. H. A. Overstreet, *The Mature Mind,* 292.
22. Thomas Merton, *The Silent Life,* 30-31.
23. "This church of the Spirit is always being built." Rufus M. Jones, *Spiritual Reformers of the Sixteenth and Seventeenth Centuries.*
24. Josiah Royce, *The World and the Individual,* I, 181.

CHAPTER VII

THE PROSPECTS TODAY

1. Pitirim A. Sorokin, *The Crisis of Our Age,* 311.
2. W. R. Inge, *Mysticism in Religion,* 136-43.
3. Sri Aurobindo, *The Life Divine,* last chapter.
4. Pitirim A. Sorokin, *The Crisis of Our Age,* 316-21.
5. Arnold J. Toynbee, *An Historian's Approach to Religion,* 236.
6. Cf. P. D. Ouspensky, in *The Psychology of Man's Possible Evolution:*
   "Man must become a different being. . . .(But) then we must understand that all men cannot develop and become different beings. . . .It may sound strange but we must realize that it is not only rare, but is becoming more and more rare. To the question: 'Why cannot all men develop and become different beings?' The answer is very simple: 'Because they do not want it'."
7. Sri Aurobindo, *The Life Divine,* last chapter.
8. Sri Aurobindo, *On Yoga,* I, 6-7.
9. Cf. George Boas, *Limits of Reason,* 153: "The rational portrait of things is an escape from the changing variety of direct experience. Its simplification is a step towards intelligibility. . . .They cannot be true to experience unless by 'true' we mean consistent. They are true to purified and

simplified experience, experience purified of its variations and simplified by the eradication of individuality."

10. The sensitives have recognized and reacted against this, Blake, Kierkegaard, Dostoevsky, for instance. Sometimes their protest has perhaps been more shrill than sound. As one of the Protestants wrote: "To hell with your System. I demand the right to behave as I like. I demand the right to regard myself as utterly unique." This, of course, is one extreme, and those who are demanding such a right may not know that the only "utterly unique" is also One-with-All.

11. In his lifetime Karl Marx is known to have said, "I am not a Marxist." What he might have said today is anybody's guess. Also think of Mahatma Gandhi and his followers.

12. In Bergson's well-known phrase. "The intellect is characterized by a natural inability to comprehend life." *Creative Evolution*, 165.

13. *See* "The transcendence of mind, which the greater physicists of the West now consider their science indicates, is the established thought-tradition in the East; and the so-called parapsychological phenomena, which have become for the last half-century the subject of psychical research in the West and which point directly to the transcendence of mind, have for ages vitally affected the intellectual outlook and the moral life of Easterns." Radhakamal Mukherji, *Theory and Practice of Mysticism*, 314.

14. *See* "The mystic, then, is not, as such a visionary, nor has he any interest in appealing to a faculty 'above reason', if reason is used in its proper sense, as the logic of the whole personality. . . .When, therefore Harnack says that 'Mysticism is nothing else than rationalism applied to the sphere above reason', he would have done better to say that it is 'reason applied to a sphere above rationalism'." W. R. Inge *Christian Mysticism*, 19, 21.

15. Alan W. Watts, *The Supreme Identity*, 40.

16. Sister Mary Francis, P. C., *A Right To Be Merry*, 6.

17. J. B. Rhine, *New World of the Mind*, 320.

18. Lecomte du Noüy, *Human Destiny*, 110.

19. Raymond B. Fosdick, *The Old Savage in the New Civilization*.

20. Arnold J. Toynbee, *An Historian's Approach to Religion*, 103-04.
21. C. A. Bennett, *A Philosophical Study of Mysticism*, 31.

Index

About the Author

SISIRKUMAR Ghose, Professor of English, Santiniketan, contributed the article on Mysticism to the fifteenth edition of *Encyclopaedia Britannica* (1974). His other works include *Aldous Huxley, The Later Poems of Tagore, The Poetry of Sri Aurobindo, Mystics and Society, Meta-esthetics and Other Essays, Modern and Otherwise, Man and Society,* and *For The Time Being.* He has also edited selections from Rabindranath Tagore, Lewis Mumford, and Arnold Toynbee.

For a complete list of Quest Books and other books published by the Theosophical Publishing House, write to:

QUEST BOOKS
306 West Geneva Road
Wheaton, Ill. 60187

We'll send you our 37 page catalog listing almost 600 titles on the following subjects:

- Asian Classics
- ESP & Clairvoyance
- Health and Diet
- Mysticism
- Religion
- Theosophy
- Astrology
- Healing
- The Human Situation
- Meditation
- Reincarnation
- Yoga
- Transpersonal Psychology